Grace in the Gray Areas

Thriving in Life's Paradoxes

KAREN KULLGREN

Grace in the Gray Areas: Thriving in Life's Paradoxes

Published by Lake Tree Press.

ISBN 9780996239806

Library of Congress Control Number 2015906512

Book Design by Brenda Hawkes

Printed in the United States of America

For my family and friends, who loved and supported me all the way

and who fill my life with grace.

And for my "Washington Woman" column readers and my blog followers,

who have reassured me there is a community for exploring

the universality of human experience together...

Table of Contents

Introduction

What is Grace in the Gray Areas? Yes, there's a play on the wisps or mops of gray hair that pop up on our heads unbidden (but well earned). But more important, what spurred me to write is my fascination with the gray areas of our lives—paradoxes where seeming opposites must be held together, decisions we must make where there is no black and white (or where there is but we have to integrate the two), expectations of one way life will be when it turns out to be another, all of these things. I think when we are very young we believe in polar opposites and very clear delineations of black and white. Only with age and wisdom do we start to see the many shades of gray we must navigate throughout our personal lives, our work, our relationships.

Even on a firm base of self-knowledge of core values, life day after day presents us with ambiguity through which we must find our way. Do we respond with faith or fear? Compassion or judgment? Acceptance or fierce revocation? Laughing or crying? Sometimes that's a gray area. Is something an opportunity or a threat? Well, sometimes, truth be told, it's both, and that's the scary and exhilarating part. What if it's good for someone else but not for me, or good for me but bad for someone else? Will this hurt someone or help them? Here is where the need for discernment comes into play.

As essayist Carolyn Knapp noted, "Our culture thrives on black-and-white narratives, clearly defined emotions, easy endings…" Grace in the Gray Areas, however, is about living with more nuanced narratives, with conflicting emotions, with complex endings. The concept of paradox, holding seeming opposites together, is central to Grace in the Gray Areas.

And what do I mean by "grace"? Divine energy, Spirit, graciousness, acceptance, kindness (to ourselves as well as others), and forgiveness are just some of its aspects.

We find gray areas in all the arenas of our lives, from our relationships with family and friends to our relationship with the divine. There is grace to be had in the gray areas between giving and receiving, between masculine and feminine, between thought and experience, between what we can control and what we cannot, between our light and shadow sides, between being human beings and being spiritual beings, on "both sides of the hard questions" (as a character in the movie *Rain Shadows* puts it), between certainty and doubt, between what is true and what is kind.

We find gray areas in time and in space as well. The middle zone of expectation of what will or should be and what is is indeed one of the great gray areas of life, and living there with grace and acceptance leads us to a far better quality of life than one constantly ruminating on what should be or what might have been. Grace in the Gray Areas is also a place where metaphors show us the way, taking us out of black and white meanings to a broader understanding of life.

Reflections

Everything I Need to Know about Life I Learn from Water Yoga

Over the years that I have been practicing water yoga, I have often been struck by how many of the things I learn about this practice offer lessons for life in general. I've spent a lot of time thinking about these metaphors and analogies.

First let me say that I am a huge proselytizer for water yoga. It makes yoga's meditative and physical benefits available to people who might not otherwise be able to do or have difficulty doing "land yoga" because of issues ranging from back problems to pregnancy to joint replacements to obesity. Anyone, from a newbie to experienced yogini, can go deeper into poses and stay in them longer in the heated water, putting less pressure on their joints. But the truth is, the real joy is that water yoga makes this overweight, middle-aged woman, grown from a childhood past of gym humiliations too numerous to mention, feel truly physically graceful for the first time.

And to boot, I learn about—

Calm in the middle of the storm: This was my first and biggest lesson, and keeps coming to me again and again in various permutations. It is a challenge sometimes, especially if we've been doing vigorous movements in the water and roiling it up, to keeping steady and balanced to do things like the Tree pose where you're standing on one leg, All you can do is still yourself from within. When you become still the water becomes still, and when each person does it, the water is peaceful and supports us all better.

Rootedness and centering: In the Tree pose, you have to press the toes of your standing leg strongly against the bottom of the pool as you raise the other leg up and bend it with your foot against the standing leg. Only then from that strong base can you raise your arms above your head to complete the pose. Just as a tree can't grow and thrive and reach the sky unless its roots are strong and deep, a person can't reach her sky, can't grow strong and tall unless she creates a deep root system for herself, of personal connections, strongly held values, and self-confidence.

Not letting uncertainty paralyze you: I often take my glasses off when I do any movements that involve putting my face in the water, and had done so in one class, but then found myself at one end of the pool going through some other asanas (poses) while my glasses were at the other end of the pool. Rather than interrupt and retrieve my glasses, I realized sometimes even when you can't see clearly doesn't mean you shouldn't still move, so I continued. You can do that in life, too, even when the path isn't clear.

The fluidity and serendipity of life: Water supports us sometimes and resists us at other times as we are still or move through it. Life can be like that, too, and we can only relax and let it move around us or give in to the buoyancy of its support. Like riptides, fighting only exhausts you and doesn't bring you back to shore.

The importance of attention and concentration: Sometimes I'm teetering to find my balance while others around me are already firmly planted. Other times I fight to hold my pose when someone next to me falls out of theirs. You have to move smoothly and stay steady even when others around you are wiggling or falling or struggling. And, of course, in yoga as in meditation as in life, if your mind wanders, bring the attention back… to the moment, to your body.

Accepting assistance: Each week while others learned and then practiced the Bow pose, Dhanurasana, I would sigh and do something else, because my knee flexibility even after surgery seemed to stop me from doing it. Then one day I decided to try and do just one side of the pose, with the better knee, and having gotten that far asked my instructor, Lakshmi, for help with my other leg, and was able to do it. That gave me the confidence and determination to keep trying and now I can do it myself! We also use foam noodles as props, and for some poses and movements hold onto the edge of the pool: there's no shame in using support.

Defying gravity: One of the most magical things about water yoga is that you are released from the chains of gravity. Poses that even for our instructor were very difficult on land become possible and comfortable in the water. Knowing now it's possible, I want to find other ways in my life to defy gravity, to be released from the chains of current realities to achieve my dreams.

Balance: Yoga places a huge emphasis on balance and complementary stretches. Every time you move your body in one pose, one direction, you must follow it with an opposite, for the good of your body, like we move in water yoga from the Cobra pose to a wall squat to reverse the stretch of our backs. Perhaps this speaks to the need for a variety of poses in and stretches of our lives to create balance, too.

Practice and determination: Another of the hugest lessons of yoga for me has been that I can, in fact, do some things I was sure I couldn't. Or there might be something I didn't think I could do but circumstances change and then I can—but I would never have known if I didn't keep trying, or try again later.

Perception and perspective: When I first started water yoga, my most hated pose, because it really hurt my shoulders, was Shalabasana, the Locust pose, where we place our noodles beneath our bellies and than fling our arms to the sky and our feet up behind us. I don't honestly know how it happened, I suppose my muscles relaxed with practice and I became more flexible, but suddenly one day the pain was gone. The pose became joyous for me, one of my favorites. Something or someone you once disliked or found impossibly difficult can become your favorite. How wonderful is that?!

Sometimes all it takes is a new perspective. I have always found difficult those poses where my arms have to do tricky things behind my back, such as a chest-opening pose where our arms are clasped together behind our backs and we're then supposed to lift them up. I never felt like I could lift them far enough or hold them in the lifted position long enough. One day, though, while floating on my back, I tried clasping my hands together beneath me and voilà, found I could push them much further away and hold that posture longer.

Adjusting expectations and adapting to limitations: We've always had people in the shifting population of my water yoga class who've had to adapt their routine because of physical issues—me, it was adapting to my arthritic knees, another young woman to chronic back problems, another to her blooming pregnancy belly, another 80-something woman to arm pain. Never before had I been in a class where I didn't want to quit if I couldn't do something as it was "supposed to be" done, but rather just fully participated doing my adaptation. The funny thing was that I'd been adapting to the limitations of my bad knees for so many years that I forgot for a while to adjust my expectations after the limitations were removed with successful surgery! Now I'm rediscovering the joys of poses I took a long time to perfect, only to lose them as my knees worsened, and I've even been able to do some poses I just couldn't do at all before the surgery. Not that there aren't a hundred more I have yet to master…

Releasing toxins: I try to let all the junk of life, all the work hassles, all the stuff on my to-do list, all the financial worries, go before class. I once told my teacher Lakshmi that on days I came in loaded with the toxic emotions or thoughts I was afraid to pollute the water with them, but she said the water would absorb them and immediately evaporate them. It eased my mind and gave me a powerful image to motivate me to leave the cares of the world at the door, or on the land, as the case may be, as I enter this sacred space where I am invited week after week to go inward.

Letting go: Oh yes, we hear a lot about the need to "let go," whether it's of our physical or mental clutter, our expectations or our need for control, and I myself have written plenty about letting go. But the other day in doing a water yoga pose where I felt uncertain and whether the noodle behind my back would support me in the water or flip me over, I had an epiphany—letting go involves trust and faith! So before anyone can be expected to let go, they've got to have trust in their support, and faith in the universe.

The real lesson is that everyone can find their gracefulness. When we give ourselves sacred space and time (for me it's an hour in a pool doing water yoga, for you it might be hours with a violin in your arms), we can feel the grace and through our silence and presence share it with others around us, too—even after we leave that space.

Paradigm Shifts

I first began thinking about paradigms, the constructs through which we view and live our lives, in reading and listening to the work of Stephen Covey.

My biggest transformational paradigm shift nearly two decades ago came not in any one great, loud epiphany, but rather in a series of quiet but important ones. Clichés became meaningful; things that I had taken for granted all my life I came to cherish. I realized that life is deeply, richly good, to be embraced and not feared. I needed to act upon my conviction that friends and family and community are more important than anything, and that expression of one's creativity is essential for happiness. I recognized something I had known all along, which is that giving is the greatest creator of meaning, the greatest form of healing.

There were myriad inputs to my changing sense of myself and of life. There were many seminal books and teachers. There was the incredible love-growing and maturing experience of parenting. A long string of career expectations and disappointments, of health challenges and scares. The struggle to preserve a failing marriage. There was my introduction to a new spiritual community, the revitalization of an old friendship, and the blossoming of several new, seemingly cosmically-ordained ones, a closer look at some family patterns and messages I received growing up. There was a steady flowing through me of a spiritual current that came straight from real life.

We often don't recognize a paradigm we're operating within until it shifts. I realized I had been viewing life as a never-ending string of problems which I was responsible for solving. I was a perfectionist who always had the highest expectations for every aspect of life, which, when the goods weren't delivered, led to chronic disappointment. Paradoxically, part of my paradigm shift was the recognition and revealing of my true self as a very optimistic person. And a huge piece was the realization that *you can change your reality by your response to it.*

So what's different for me now? I greet each day as a gift (and like receiving a gift, when I open the package, even if I don't like it, I smile and accept it). I try to condition each encounter I have with another human being with kindness, whether I know them or not (and sometimes when I know them it's even harder). I try to assume the best about people and events rather than the worst, and put myself in their shoes. I know there are many things more important than being right, or perfect—compassion and good mental health among them. Two things that flow from these attitudes are increased tolerance and a greater capacity for forgiveness. Of myself, and others. And there's a ripple effect—when you start seeing people differently, behaving towards them differently, sometimes they start thinking of and behaving towards you differently, too.

In some cases what flowed from the shift was easy, in other cases difficult. Patterns were deeply etched, habits needed to be broken. The follow-through is an ongoing process, the success of which is measured daily. But I gave myself permission not to be perfect, promised not to beat myself up when I slipped. One critical element of my paradigm shift was letting go. I gave up control, or, more accurately, gave up the perspective that I could or should control everything around me. Giving up control is not to say that I let fate buffet me entirely, and giving up worrying as a way of life does not mean I don't take sensible precautions. But I try to relax and take things as they come. And I usually have the good sense to recognize when a path I'm doggedly plodding down to no effect is, perhaps, the wrong path, or that I will get where I'm heading when life is damn good and ready.

There have always been people in my life who were so alive yet so unflappable they just drove me nuts. While I won't say I've become unflappable, I definitely choose my flaps more carefully! It has been a long process of seeing, absorbing, weighing, this is who I want to be, this is what I don't want to do, and yes, a process that includes making mistakes.

A paradigm shift creates a shift in energy and new possibilities. Readiness and an open mind are the fertile soil for that; so is love, and so is loss. I have to keep reminding myself of that, as I continue to forge my path to authentic existence.

Innie or Outie?

I have two sides, two aspects to my personality that are held uncomfortably together sometimes while other times one pushes into dominance.

I am an introvert *and* an extrovert. I can be quite convivial, vivacious even, at social events of a not-too- overwhelming size. Other times I could draw a box around myself perhaps six feet out on all sides and be happy to walk in the world with my privacy intact. Yet other times I remove myself from the game entirely and shut down in my free time, staying in and trying to recharge in solitude.

I tend to gravitate to others who also have this mixed state, who will sometimes become almost hermitic when life becomes overwhelming. Though I understand it, it can also hurt if I am in a reaching- out mode and they are in a turning-in mode. We each take our chances.

My oh-so Western desire for privacy and space has been particularly challenged over the years in my forays into the Asian world. When I was straight out of college off to Taipei, Taiwan for a year, I was fortunately able to kick the social me into hyperdrive. A good thing, too, for personal space and privacy are entirely alien concepts in Asian culture. I took my time there to be some magical adventure and was wide open to it all—the crowds, the cacophony, the pollution, the crazy traffic, the pulsing beat of the city, and the astonishing warmth of people. Nearly two decades later I had a very different experience of living in Tianjin, which was one of the most densely populated and most polluted cities in the world. Then I found the stares and the complete inability to set foot out the door without being gawked at and even followed, whether lacking in malice or not, completely intolerable. Eventually I became nearly agoraphobic.

My ex-husband, who is Chinese, was never able to understand the side of me that sometimes craves privacy and space. I was expected to be open to last-minute company and invasive requests 24/7 and woe to me if I wasn't, for then I was accused of being "selfish," the harshest judgment he could bring to bear.

Now, I walk precariously on the tightrope between my interior world and my exterior world. I have worked from home for 17 years now, eight of them alone since my son left for college. Most of my work is by email and phone, which sometimes suits me fine and gives me some small measure of control in a very chaotic work environment. Other times I feel painfully isolated. Aware of a tendency to sink into depression if I don't get out some (though equally possible if I don't get enough solitude), at one point last summer I became a social butterfly, going to singles events every weekend, and loving it. This summer I feel too easily overstimulated, and choose my outings more carefully, usually preferring time with close friends that allows for quiet conversation over mob scene happy hours for which invitations roll into my email inbox every week. I'm going for quality, not quantity, and planting my roots deep rather than shallow. I don't enjoy big festivals much—don't like the crowds, but still sometimes have to force myself out.

So here I sit most happily at poolside in my neighborhood on a hot Sunday afternoon, after floating around in the water for an hour, now reading and writing. I've seen one of my son's best friends, which I always like because it connects me to a time gone by (I actually think I see more of him than my own son these days, as he still lives in the neighborhood). Next to me a woman I lived on a cul de sac with—our dogs were friends—has plopped down to read in companionable silence, and another neighbor stops by to catch up. There's a not-unpleasant background buzz of kids playing and splashing about, and parents who move from joining in the play to flattening onto a chaise for some sun. The sky is blue, blue, blue with just a puff of white cloud here and there. The gorgeous, mature trees around the outer edges create some shade and breeze, but don't block the sun from the center. The European lifeguards enjoy their last few weeks here before returning to their home countries for the school year.

I am surrounded by people but alone, perfectly at peace, enjoying the summer too soon to come to a close, holding my introvert-cum-extrovert self, for one afternoon, in balance.

Meditation "Challenge"—They're Not Kidding

I'm watching a DVR'd episode of Dr. Oz and Deepak Chopra is his guest. Chopra leads Oz and the audience in studio and at home in a short meditation to demonstrate the stilling and relaxing power of the practice. Now, I've tried meditation over the years (Radical Acceptance with Tara Brach, Insight Meditation with Sharon Salzberg, private lessons with a guy who was trying to impress me in college) and it's never "taken." I've definitely felt the meditative quality of things like my water yoga, and simply stopping and remembering to breathe in the middle of my day, in the middle of a stressful event. Yet neither group meditation practice nor meditation CDs have done it for me. But for these five minutes on a TV show of all things, I listen and I breathe and I go to a deeper place.

Then just a couple of weeks later I read a friend's blog talking about how wonderful she felt after completing the Chopra Center 21 Day Meditation Challenge. Obviously the universe is sending me a message. In one of those classic post-New Year's attempts at redemption, I decide it's time to start a meditation practice! I go to the Chopra Center website and sign up for emails that will soon start coming to my inbox, with daily guided meditations.

Day 1—The challenge starts without me as I am on a much-deserved, all-too-brief vacation and have disconnected from the Internet.

Day 2-7—I can't start, I realize, because the speakers on my desktop computer haven't worked since one of last year's Snowmaggedon power outages.

Day 8—After trying everything for a DIY fix to my speakers, I call Fuji (manufacturer of the monitor they're built into). Am told if speakers aren't working it's not worth trying to repair them—I should go buy some external speakers. Now they tell me!

Day 9—**My Day 1**. No time to go shopping for speakers. I do the challenge after work, on my laptop downstairs. Feel very virtuous.

Their Day 10, **My Day 2.** Topic: "The Centering Power of the Breath." I fall asleep during the meditation in my recliner.

Their Day 11, **My Day 3.** I go get speakers at Target. Cheap—why did I wait so long to take care of this problem?

My Day 5. I am not connecting with the different person guiding today's meditation, even though I'm told he's called "the Boston Buddha," which normally would warm me to him.

Two days in a row my days were so busy that I didn't do the meditations till after work. It's dark out. I'm burned out. I am hungry. I am a disgrace to the program. I am so antsy I fast forward through the guided meditation. Pretty sure this is not what they had in mind.

Think I might do better on my own just sitting in my chair doing a five-minute meditation, and build up the time as best I can, rather than be a slave to the computer, to my inbox, and to the messages from Chopra Center telling me what meditation is and isn't. I appreciate that some people need this. For me I think it's an obstacle. I've never been a groupie for meditation. It's like the biggest, very popular meditation community in our area, meeting weekly in a local church. For me that would involve driving at least 30 minutes (on a good day, if rush hour is over), then taking 20 minutes to find remote parking and trek from it to the church, and by then in a horrible mood go join 300 other people and all the stuff they bring to sit together. I just never got it.

The Day 21 message comes into my email urging participants to celebrate. I scroll back to Day 8, which is where I am. I want to get this over with. Not a good attitude, I know. But tonight I wait a little longer, because it's close to 6 p.m., and, wait for it, there's the glorious sunset behind the trees across the lake, wide swatches of pink and blue defining the bare branches where the tree line thins. This is what I really need to meditate to, with eyes wide open.

The pink is heading south and the blue is fading to gray then black, and now I feel the letdown that comes as the day fades into night. There's so little daylight this winter, I hate to close my eyes for 10-15 minutes of it. But if I wait till night time in the dark to meditate, it makes me sleepy or just feels too late. Ironically, the title of today's Challenge for me is "Create a Morning Meditation Ritual." This depressing winter, just getting up is enough of a morning ritual challenge!

Today's meditation starts off indeed with a challenge—telling us that the reason most people stop meditating is that they "don't have enough time." Er, guilty! Then the guide mentions that we might be thinking of taxes and damn, now I'm thinking of my taxes, papers for which are strewn across my dining room table! Why? Why remind me of taxes when I'm trying to settle into a quiet, spiritual place? I have my own inner voices, I don't need anyone planting noise there just as I'm trying to get rid of it.

Now that the challenge has formally ended (for everyone else—though I still have 13 more days to go), emails continue to pour into my inbox from the Chopra Center. A new radio program I can listen to, a meditation CD I can buy, a retreat I can attend. Support, or commercialism? Maybe equal parts of each.

Still, I'll probably try, in my lackadaisical way, to finish all 21 days. After all, they promise to help me variously find out who I am, see what I want, discover my purpose, open my chakras, and achieve effortless flow. Who can possibly resist that?

Do-Overs

A friend recently had a serious car crash (she was okay, but her car wasn't). As she pondered what replacement to get with the insurance money, she remarked that she really just wanted to get the same car she had—a sporty little convertible. And indeed she went with her heart and got herself another just like it. Somehow this idea of embracing what she called "a do-over" really stuck with me on a deeper level.

I like the concept of a do-over. Transformation. Second chances. Is life an unlimited menu of do-overs, with only our internal constraints stopping us from taking the reins?

The ultimate modern do-over, Liquid Paper, was invented by a secretary in Texas a little over 50 years ago. (The original name was "Mistake Out.") Before personal computers, when we had those ubiquitous white bottles in every desk drawer, what did we do when an idea or turn of phrase turned out not to be brilliant, when a typewriter key had a mind of its own, when our weary hands stumbled? We had to either erase messily or plunge on with a quick penstroke correction that was forgiving of our error, or we had to rip the page out and start over. Two approaches, then, to the do-over, one to make course corrections as you go along, fluidly, the other a more radical rejection and starting again.

If we started asking the universe for real do-overs, how much would we be willing to risk? How much would we be willing to lose? Of course some of the things we'd take a do-over on are things that in fact we just didn't have the maturity, the money, the time, the wisdom to do differently originally. Definitely there's that old chestnut, "youth is wasted on the young." And if we're playing this game fairly, taking a do-over means that all the things that happened because of that "mistake" we made earlier on don't happen either, right? Do we really want it to be about do-overs or do we want to live with the consequences of our choices?

Like so many divorced moms, I can't regret my marriage because without it I wouldn't have my son exactly as he is, 100% perfectly himself, as the offspring of that man and me in the time and place we were together. I can't regret living in places I didn't like, because I made friends in those places; I learned things about myself. I can't regret bad jobs and bad bosses because they tested my mettle, and taught me what was not right for me, which, after all, is as important as knowing what is right, and a necessary step to getting to that knowledge.

I've been asking women about their own do-overs. A lot of them harkened back to their 20s. Some betray anger at parents, others wistfulness for dreams deferred, others bitterness over a relationship. One educational administrator said she wouldn't have let her mother dissuade her from pursuing her dream to become a professional actress. One non-profit executive said she would have earlier on realized that as well as respecting other people's spiritual belief systems, she had to respect her own. A mother said she would have only taken a leave of absence from her high-powered job rather than quit when she became unhappy at work and stressed at home. A grandmother said, "While I wanted marriage and children, I would have trusted no man with my life." A retired educator wanted to have become a professional athlete, and as long as she was in do-over mode, she wanted to play tennis with Billie Jean King, too!

A 50-year-old woman who has happily step-parented her partner's several grown children wonders if she should have more seriously considered becoming a mother herself. Her definite do-over would be having worked harder on her relationship with her late mother. A frustrated artist said she'd love to be a student again, auditing courses on a non-degree basis for fun. Of her marriage, she said, "I wouldn't simply exist as long as I did thinking I had to."

Several women of various ages said if they had it to do over they would have become more strategic about finances earlier on. My mom asked for do-overs on a variety of fronts ranging from jobs to cars, adding, "I wouldn't have worn high heels in high school and college and ruined my feet!"

The most poignant of wishes for a chance to do something differently came from a woman I have only known as a deeply compassionate adult. She shared a secret memory of herself as a young child who one day betrayed a friend by treating the friend unkindly, because the little girl was different, and because the other kids egged her on. "I felt such shame and realized I'd sold my soul," she told me. "I wasn't mature enough to know what to do. I'd like a do-over more than anything."

Some authors write their novels according to a precise outline. I think some of us view our lives like that. But I have come to understand that life for most of us unfolds much more organically. If we're flexible and hopeful enough, maybe it's really never too late for a do-over. As my wise friend Laura said, "I'm laying the groundwork for a happy old woman who can say she lived life as she wanted."

Blessing Adversity

A basic tenet of Buddhism is that if something comes into your attention, it has something to teach you, and I believe that. Not that I'm recommending looking for trouble as a path for spiritual growth. Don't worry—trouble will find you.

I've been thinking about adversity a lot lately as I, my family, my community, my country, and my world face imposing challenges to our economy, to our livelihoods, to our faith. I look at adversity as a beginning, not an end. However painful the challenges presented to us, whether of catastrophic proportions like a death or a devastating curve ball like a job loss or just one of the "one thing after another" we sometimes face, we have choices in how we move forward. I in no way mean to diminish anyone's grief, or anger, or disappointment, or fear. But while we cannot necessarily control or determine a particular outcome, we can, eventually, control our own response.

Adversity makes us think; it makes us examine and re-examine our lives. The meaning of something bad happening may not be apparent until years later, if ever. I try, when I have gone through a difficult experience, to find at least one good thing that came of it, big or small. This invariably comforts me. A surgery years ago, preceded by weeks of considerable pain, made me realize how much I loved my neighborhood and how much I could count on my friends and family, as casseroles poured into the house, rides were offered, my yucky dressings were changed, and my son was cared for by others. Leaving my "dream job" precipitated a re-examination of my life that led to redefining myself as a writer. A year in China, in a dark industrial city where I plunged into depression and feared for my son's and my health in the polluted environment, brought me new friends from around the world. It made me snap to attention about environmental health issues, it made me appreciate every tree in my yard, in my community, tenfold, and it also made me fiercely protective of the rights and obligations of our country's democratic tradition.

The lessons of my knee surgery are still fresh. Not being able to walk properly for many weeks was a wake-up call to take responsibility for my health, a reminder to be compassionate to the obvious and hidden pain of others and to be tolerant of the slow-moving in our midst. I appreciate the completely taken-for-granted knees that support each step I have taken through the world. And metaphorically, I learned about resilience. As Robin Morgan wrote in *Upstairs in the Garden*, "Blessed be my knees that I may bend so as not to break."

There are some other challenges I have faced or am facing whose blessings I am still sorting out. But I am comforted that there is meaning, whether or not it is revealed to me, and try not to be mired in bitterness over the past but grounded in the present.

So what are the blessings of adversity?

Adversity represents a rebirth, an opportunity for change and growth. The enemy of stasis, adversity challenges us to action, whether that means quiet changes we make in our personal lives or more public stands we take.

Adversity reminds us of our riches, and of the importance of gratitude for so much that we take for granted, most of all the preciousness of each and every moment and day that we are given.

Adversity teaches us mindfulness; it teaches us to *pay attention.*

Adversity renews our compassion, as we learn what it is to walk in another's shoes.

Surviving adversity, and coming through at the other end, gives us hope and a renewed commitment to life.

Adversity teaches us acceptance.

Adversity shows us the importance of friendship and community.

As I finish writing this, I pick up my daily newspaper, with the business section talking about how credit card companies are putting the squeeze on people, the metro section headed by a story of local senior citizens remembering the Great Depression and its parallels to today, the front page article on world leaders meeting on the economic crisis—and the dread again overtakes me. I fear for my present and future and those of my family and my country.

But I'm sticking to my story. Adversity can reveal to us our own strength and the innate strength and optimism of humanity. Albert Camus wrote, "In the midst of winter, I found there was within me an invincible summer." I have faith in that; in this wintry time, I am trying hard to find my inner summer.

Lighting the Dark

For I can see that in the midst of death life persists, in the midst of untruth, truth persists, in the midst of darkness light persists.

—Mohandas Gandhi

The sun is out today. Still a startling rarity after dark days of nearly nonstop rain that made us forgot all complaints of a hot summer. A crazy summer all over our country—fire, drought, heat waves, flooding, a mid-Atlantic earthquake. Mother Nature is acting out our human woes on a grand scale.

We are out of work. We are losing our homes. We can't get treated properly for our illnesses because we can't afford it. We are struggling to put food on the table for our children, if indeed we are lucky enough to have a table. Teachers fight to give our children a good education in inadequate facilities with inadequate budgets even for books in some cities. Crops are decimated, and precious animals are in danger of becoming extinct. We work twice as hard and twice as many hours for the same or half the pay. Americans are choosing between food and healthcare.

And today, September 11, 2011, we commemorate an unthinkable tragedy, an unprecedented assault on American soil, ten years ago but just a blink away in our memories.

In all this dark, where is the light?

In the pond out my window, adult geese and ducks glide across the surface with their goslings and ducklings. A great blue heron soars to the very top of a tall tree. I walk out of my house and a squirrel just outside that just nabbed a nut somewhere in the woods (and is bringing it to hide in one of the container plants I keep out front, to dig up in winter) freezes, thinking perhaps if he doesn't move I won't notice him. I greet him, and the birds hopping nearby for seeds, and assure them I mean them no harm. This simple ritual, repeated day after day to squirrels, birds, and chipmunks alike, makes me very happy.

I drive out of my driveway and wave hello to one or the other of my neighbors out walking their dogs, and if I'm not rushing to an appointment, I slow and roll down the window for a more personal hello. If I'm very lucky before I even get into my car I run into my favorite beagle, Penny (and her owner) and get some doggie love from this precocious canine. (If I somehow miss her, I still can revel in her antics on her "mom's" Facebook page, with daily sharing of her pet's mischief.)

I go to my town center, and cross the square where kids are scrambling up and down the boulders put out for that purpose, and people of every age and color stroll, and if I'm very lucky it's a night with free music in the square. I head into my neighborhood library, and, well, everyone knows what a land of enchantment a library is, don't they? I am like a kid in a candy store—in awe of all the choices, all the stories housed there that will transport me to another country, another time, another great author's imagination or memory, for escape, deeper insight, or good laughs.

I go to a local swim center where for 45 minutes a day I am enveloped in the warm womb of the water. I jump around in my water exercise class and celebrate my body's flexibility and agility where gravity is not my enemy. I admire my much older classmates who are there celebrating their bodies, too, in their 60s, 70s, 80s even, reassuring me that the water will always be my haven and exercise always available to me.

Everywhere I go, despite their personal troubles, people still smile as they pass one another on the street, in the halls. When I'm feeling really down, a smile from a stranger goes a long, long way. I pay it forward as often as I can. We're all putting one foot in front of the other, doing our best, navigating a confusing, changing way of life in a time where, the newspaper just informed me, one in three Americans my age are living in reduced economic circumstances from the previous generation. It's in stark contrast to the obscene wealth that somehow persists in some communities in our area. But rich or poor, we all have our trials.

And we all get up each morning to a new chance at life, a new hope of things improving, a new opportunity to be with the people we love, and a new urge to smile at strangers as we pass, or better still, stop and say hello and see how we might help one another. And remember a day of great sacrifice that, in so many ways then and since, called on us to bring out our best selves.

Time and Attention

Multitasking

I used to proudly flaunt my multitasking skills on my résumé. Now I think multitasking is a dirty word.

Realistically I know that we live in a world that runs on deadlines. This I can accept. The constant race for bigger and better I'm afraid I no longer do. The unrealistic amount of output expected by a given deadline in the face of reduced resources, reduced time, increased competition, and way too plugged-in technology makes all this multitasking feel like, well, a rat race. Upping our consumption of anti-anxiety medications just isn't going to cut it. A more radical approach is required.

Let's start this summer. I challenge those of you going on a summer vacation to leave behind your laptops and PDAs, and ask your boss and colleagues not to call or email you unless your office is on fire. And don't pick up a newspaper or watch TV. I won't either. What will that be like? Hopefully, we will have a vacation focused on where we are and who we are with. And you know what? All those things you ignored? They'll still be going on when you get back. All those things on your to-do list? You can tackle them then—one at a time.

We have become a society of scatterbrains. We are overloaded adults, overprogrammed kids. We are asked to simultaneously not only receive limitless amounts of information from everything from personal contact to smartphones to television to computers, but interact with those media, too. My son and his classmates were whizzes at doing homework while texting, flipping channels on the TV, and discussing what the teacher meant by this assignment on the phone at the same time—while eating. Maybe youth are hardwired for overload these days, but surely that can't be good.

All of our connectivity, our cell phones, emails, give an absurdly inflated sense of urgency to every business communication. Slow down already! Be patient! I can't help but wonder—don't we deserve to just be "out of touch" once in a while?

Sometimes I feel like I'm juggling so many things at one time that my mind is going too fast for my mouth to keep up, and I can hardly string together a coherent sentence. Musician Cliff Eberhardt spoke to this phenomenon with an anecdote about a song he was introducing. It was about a couple who was separated by an international border, but recently, he said, he introduced it absent-mindedly as about a couple "separated by an International House of Pancakes." "I'm always thinking about the next thing," he said with a rueful laugh.

In the midst of a work crunch, it's the hardest—but most necessary—to go back to Stephen Covey (*The Seven Habits of Highly Effective People*, *First Things First*) and his recommended sorting of "urgent" vs. "important." When I don't, I find that, sadly, "important" gets very short shrift in my own life. It's like the parable he tells. Take a large jar and try and fill it with pebbles and large rocks. What happens if you put all the pebbles in first? No room for the large rocks. You have to put the large rocks—the truly "important" stuff of your life, whether that be your values, your family, your creativity, whatever—in first; then the pebbles, the little stuff, can fill in the spaces around that.

We may have to take absurd measures to switch to unitasking. To force my attention to something that kept getting back-burnered, on the way out of the grocery store I had to pull out my cell phone and leave myself a message on my work phone to put aside everything else on my desk the next morning and just do it, admonishing myself by voice mail—"This is important, Karen!" So I did it. And it felt great. And the world did not end and deadlines were not missed, clients were not lost, the other things that required my attention did not crash and burn—they simply waited, for one measly, precious hour. Here's a little secret. No one will encourage you to do one thing at a time—not your boss, your clients, your family. You have to do it for yourself.

Unitasking is very liberating. When your adrenaline's pumping as you multitask 'til the stress threatens to make you burst, and you're crabby and crazy, all you have to do is STOP, right now, everything except one thing. One thing at a time. Take a deep breath. Then repeat after me, "All is well." The feeling of spaciousness is immediate.

In a town where people's regard for us and our regard for ourselves is often based on what we do, might it be time to focus on being instead of doing?

A Lazy Thought

There go the grown ups
To the office,
To the store.
Subway rush,
Traffic crush;
Hurry, scurry,
Worry, flurry.
No wonder
Grownups
Don't grow up
Any more.
It takes a lot
Of slow
To grow.

—Eve Merriam

The Beast of Busyness

I am not superwoman. I cannot do it all. I must stop trying to do it all. I must slow down.

It's hard. It's really hard. I can write these words, I can write columns on the subject and know in my mind and my heart that it's true, but why is it then that I still slide back into and struggle anew out of the abyss of excessive busyness, of multitasking (which I still believe is a dirty word)?

It's not just me. It's every woman I know, married or single, with children or not, in her 30s or in her 60s. Ask someone, "How are you?" and they answer "busy" or "crazed" or "slammed at work." I used to love how a friend would instead of "too busy" say her life was "abundant," and I started saying it too. But I'm not saying it anymore. Because what I'm experiencing isn't abundance—and her life has become so abundant her friends don't see much of her any more.

It's not just bad for our mental health. It's bad for our physical health. It's bad for our spiritual health. It's bad for our productivity, our clients, our relationships with colleagues; it's bad for business. It's gotten worse with the economy the way it is and with the technology we thought would save us spurring us only to higher expectations of productivity and constant over-availability.

I hear myself telling people I feel like "a rat on a treadmill" or a "hamster on a wheel" and I cringe. We are overcommitted and overstretched, and we are certainly ourselves not without blame. And as has been much chronicled in recent years—but has not changed one iota except in acceleration—we've let our kids become infected with the disease of busyness, too, from their overscheduled extracurricular lives to their ever-plugged-in short attention spans.

I walk a very fine line, as do many women I know, between introverted and extroverted, between the need to be social and engaged and the need for down time. One friend who recently adopted a child loves being a mom but is flabbergasted at the loss of what little free time she once had. Even with a support system most parents would envy, caring for a toddler fills up every waking moment. Another woman, trying to build her dream alternative healing practice, juggles three jobs to support that and only barely makes time for her religious community, with no time for a social life. And another woman I know finds her time happily but overabundantly full of caring for her grandchildren to help her overstressed children out.

Sometimes we struggle so hard with the balancing act that we overcompensate and shut down entirely, shutting out friends, social engagements, community connections. As authors Jacqueline Olds, MD and Richard S. Schwartz, MD argue in *The Lonely American: Drifting Apart in the Twenty-first Century*, "A web of relationships is like the hammock that holds a person safely above the hard ground of depression; a web of relationships is also like a snare that holds a person back from the freshness of possibilities. It's never easy to get the balance right, but when a person sheds too many obligations because they feel more like a snare than a hammock, he may shed the very connections that keep him from going to ground."

I have to push myself out the door many times even to social events at which I know I'll have a great time. But I need to see my friends and family, who keep me sane and whole. And my work situation is quite isolating—well, as a pal in a similar situation laughs, if we don't force ourselves out, the only way we'll ever find a soulmate is if he's delivering a package or coming to unplug the sink.

It's funny (funny sad, not funny ha-ha) the ways we capture all the "shoulds" in our lives—on BlackBerries, on Post-its that litter our desks and our dashboards, on "to-do" lists tucked in our purses, or, in my case, notes I've written in the middle of the night then thrown on the bedroom floor as I drift off and suddenly remember something that has to get taken care of the next day. We're "shoulding ourselves to death," as the wise-beyond-her-years Carrie Bradshaw once wrote on "Sex and the City." Even things that used to bring us joy become burdens. Taking a much needed vacation, if we have the financial luxury to do so, seems impossible when we feel under so much pressure to get things done before we leave and know we will be slammed with catching up once we get back.

I fretted about the financial drain of a recent decision to hire some help for my home office. And then my old friend Cathy emailed me, "You can always get some more money, but once you've lost your mind, well, that's pretty much it." WOW!!! That was my epiphany, my "aha" moment.

Hint for each day: B—r—e—a—t—h—e... (What kind of a world do we live in that we need to remind each other to breathe?!)

Hurry Up and Slow Down

I've had enough—haven't you? Life shouldn't be nonstop frenzy. It's time to slow down.

I reached deep down inside myself and set it in motion—or, rather, in slow motion. Like any life change, it's a work in progress, a daily practice, and some days I am better at it than others. Here are some lessons I've learned, tools I've taken up to help me slow down.

We women talk a good game about taking care of ourselves, but when it comes right down to it, it falls way down on our priority lists, behind family responsibilities, work, and other obligations. And we still feel somehow guilty about it. What Suzanne Braun Levine astutely points out in her book, *Fifty is the New Fifty: 10 Life Lessons for Women in Second Adulthood,* applies to women of any age. "Reclaiming our time, our concentration, our privacy is a first step toward doing unto ourselves" as we are always doing unto/for others. Putting ourselves first really just means putting ourselves up as high on the list as everyone and everything else.

The bottom line is that our bosses are never going to tell us to slow down. The strapped nonprofits where we volunteer are never going to say, "Don't worry, we'll find someone else for the committee this year." Our children are never going to say, "Don't worry, you take a bath and read a book, we'll play quietly here by ourselves and won't bother you." We are the only ones who can do it. We are the only ones who can calm ourselves in the middle of the storm long enough to make changes in our routines and changes in our attitudes.

"Hurry is a form of violence exercised upon time," said Donald Nicholl, a religious scholar. We need to stop doing violence to precious resources like time, and our physical and mental health and our spirits.

If we don't identify our own big-picture life priorities and live accordingly, we will spend our lives in a constant state of reaction and heedless hurry rather than creation with intention and purpose.

Lowering or releasing our expectations may be shocking notions to overachiever Americans, but they're the only paths to serenity. "Let It Be" and "Let Go" are worthy mantras.

Remember, we can't really control what happens, only our response to it.

Everything doesn't have to be perfect. Accept "good enough" (including from ourselves and others).

We need to stop overcommitting ourselves. Or as Suzanne Braun Levine puts it, "*No* is Not a Four Letter Word." Sometimes to protect our own need for a slower pace we have to say no to others. Other times we have to say no to ourselves—our need to please, our desire to help, our urge to fix things.

Traffic trials, daily annoyances, and pet peeves are *so* not worth our attention. "Don't sweat the small stuff" may be trite, but it's true. Don't wait for a nasty wake-up call (a health crisis, a job loss, etc.) to put things in perspective.

Reducing consumption isn't just eco-friendly, it's also a way to lighten your load. The less we bring into our homes and our lives, the less we have to tend to it rather than tending to ourselves, our relationships, our communities. Think twice about that tantalizing item on the shelf, on your computer screen. Is it worth adding as baggage to your journey through life?

Time management and endless striving for organization aren't real solutions. I suspect that the push, external or internal, to become more and more organized and efficient is just a fool's errand—an attempt to make order out of chaos, to have the illusion of control over the inherently unruliness of work, of relationships, of parenting, of life. "Manage" your time, like your closet, by filling it with less stuff.

Buddhists focus on our need to be present, mindful, and "in the moment." I'm all for that, for the most part. But maybe sometimes we just need to stop some meaningless task and let our minds be carried away instead to the woods or the lake. Maybe, after all, we sometimes need to get *out* of the moment, not be *in* it.

A quote I keep from Gandhi reminds me, "There is more to life than increasing its speed." In one of life's little paradoxes, one of those gray areas that so fascinate me, by slowing down we often actually become more effective. In addition to creating space for things like reflection, growth, and joy.

Mixed Bag

The Library Lover

A book I was reading late one night mentions a woman in a library. Suddenly, I'm transported decades back to the small, historic New England town library where I spent much of my childhood. I grew up there, in the town, yes, but perhaps even more so in that library where I spent so many hours browsing and reading, and whose bounty I brought home to transport me to worlds far away.

At the back of the upper floor were the main adult stacks. Every letter of the alphabet beckoned with a thrill. On the first aisle to the right, I pulled down every book by Pearl Buck, Agatha Christie, Ian Fleming, Erle Stanley Gardner. On the first aisle to the left I found Rachel Carson's *Silent Spring* and on the second aisle the riches of the travel books, which also exposed me to adventurous women, from Emily Hahn to Cornelia Otis Skinner. Back to the left was the Dag Hammarskjöld book on the UN. Far to the right rear was *A Tree Grows in Brooklyn.* I shared with my father a love of Robert Ludlum books back when Bourne was a character in a book, not a film series with Matt Damon. I traveled back to the Hawaii of centuries ago and crossed a Mideast desert in a caravan with James Michener. All of these and many volumes more shaped my future adult sensibilities.

Will the places the Internet can take young people ever replace the vast worlds inside that small public library?

At the middle of the stacks on the back wall was that much loved (by me, at least), mammoth precursor to the PC, the mighty card catalog. Drawer after drawer of index cards on thousands of books, the card catalog was the key that unlocked the great treasures of the library.

At the circulation desk there was always one of several women with eyeglasses, hair in buns, cardigans over their shoulders, playing keepers of the gate. Despite their stern demeanor if you were a library patron imprudent enough to raise your voice in that sacred space, they also were my heroes.

My mind jumps back further still to the lower floor of the library. To the left, the young children's room, where the magic of *The Secret Garden*, *Mary Poppins*, *Caddie Woodlawn,* and all the *Oz* books captivated me, and the *We Were There* books were my earliest entrees into history. The picture book section enchanted me even after I was older, with *The Story of Babar: The Little Elephant*, *The Lonely Doll*, *The Five Chinese Brothers* (not at all politically correct now), and another whose title escapes me but I remember in a fond blur, involving a truck full of turnips.

In time, I moved out to the older children's and teen's room, where the furniture got taller and the books expanded my world even further, where I discovered the wilderness with *White Fang* and my keenness for mysteries with Nancy Drew.

I used to want to become a librarian, but realize that what I would have loved—helping people find a book they or their children would love or needed—has become a more hands-off exercise involving database searches, less so a friendly face at the information desk who would pore over the shelves with you, touching volumes reverently before pulling one or two off triumphantly to hand to you. I suppose today's library is more democratic, as there really is no more gatekeeper, but I miss those days nonetheless.

I am saddened by the fact that my son is not a Library Lover like his mother. Yes, I took him to the library from the time he was an infant: we took out stacks of books and attended story times, and I read to him and he read to me for years. It isn't that he doesn't love to read. But for research, instead of going to the library, he goes to the Internet, and his college library was a place for quiet study rather than the glory of books. For pleasure reading, he used to go to the bookstore; now he just orders online for his iPad. Perhaps when he has children of his own he will rediscover and remember his youthful enchantment with the library as a place where you can not only find what you're looking for but stumble upon surprise after surprise.

The town I live in now has a brand-new, huge library, with a massive atrium soaring up to the second floor. I miss the cozier feeling of a smaller library, though I'm sure the employees are happy to have the larger, updated space. It's the closest library to me, but I often go instead to one farther away where I can still park near the door and lug a heavy bag of books in to return and out to take home and devour, where the ceilings are lower and the furniture older, but the feeling of magic is somehow still more present.

I yearn to go back to my childhood library but fear I would be disappointed. I just went to the library's website, though, and found this mission statement: "to enrich the community by connecting people to the world of ideas, information and imagination in order to support their work, education, personal growth and enjoyment." Perhaps I would still be right at home there after all.

Casual Sundays

Anyone who knows me very well knows that I am normally loathe to make plans on a Sunday. Sunday is my shut-down, re-center, recharge day. When I'm feeling contemplative, I call it Sabbath. But mostly, I just call it like it is. Pajama Day.

There are two key elements to Pajama Day. No, make that three.

No bra required.

Sleeping in, not setting the alarm.

Nothing planned, don't have to be anyplace, don't have to do anything for anybody!

Having said that, yes, I may do laundry, and I definitely have to take out the trash and recycling (a task for which I wait for night to fall, then throw a coat over my PJs and skulk out under cover of darkness). And there's usually at least one article that needs to be written.

But I had this epiphany that the pajama (or, in summer, night shirt) aspect of Pajama Day isn't just about being comfortable.

It's also about not having to make any choices, even about something as simple as what to wear. (Contrary to common belief about people who work from home offices, I do get dressed in clothes every work day.) We have to use judgment when we get dressed, based on myriad criteria we don't even realize we're using. What's the temperature outside? What's the temperature inside? Which of my clothes are clean? Which are a little dirty but no one has to know? Which clothes do I have to save to be clean for an event later in the week? Can I handle a tight waistline today or not?

My life has become so paralyzed by choices I can't make just one more. There is no discernment involved in reaching into my drawer—or onto the floor by my bed—for PJs. Done, and done.

All week all I do is multitask, and make choices, and filter information coming at me from 60 directions. I juggle service to my clients and my employers. I interact with my family and friends (hopefully in a loving and compassionate way); I help those around me who need help. I decide not just about things that are a chore but things that are fun. What am I doing on Saturday? Are we going to eat out before that event or not? If so, where should we go? Where will we park? What time do we need to leave by to get where we're going in time? Can I afford it? Will they have something I can eat that's both healthy and delicious? (Relative weight given to each depending on what day you ask me.) I triage problems ranging from work on my car or house to scheduling doctor's appointments. At the grocery store I literally become dazed by all the choices around me, brands, packaging, health benefits real or perceived, label-reading, what things will I put together to make each meal, how long will these veggies last? Ay yay yay, day in and day out, my head is spinning!

But Sunday? Sunday? No. I refuse. I figure if I pull my boundaries in tight around me, in this case the walls and windows of my living room, there will be less pulling at my attention, fewer choices to make. Maybe I can keep my wits about me.

Of course, Washington, DC's notoriously mercurial spring is putting a bit of a glitch in my no-choices-on-Sunday resolve. I came downstairs today having shifted to my "shoulder season" pajamas in a lighter fabric, having moved from winter flannels but not ready for a short cotton nightshirt. One toe out the door to get the *Post* on my front walk, and I knew the TV meteorologists had lied; it was not that warm out. I tromped back upstairs to grab my flannel PJs. And I chose—to take them out for one more spin.

Body Image

I have been preoccupied in recent years with the challenges of living an authentic life. I've come to realize it requires co-existing with the gray areas not only of our hair but of our humanity—about living with, even embracing, all its glorious, frustrating ambiguity. 'Tis the (swimsuit) season for baring it all, and in that spirit I thought I'd revisit a topic that screams ambiguity—women and our bodies.

C.S. Lewis said: "You don't have a Soul. You *are* a Soul. You have a body." If we look at our bodies as temples, then is it surprising we decorate with such abandon and worry when some of the roof tiles become discolored or hinges rusty?

As smart modern women who know that real beauty comes from within, should we castigate ourselves when we want to "look nice," for ourselves, for others? Why do I feel guilty when I open up my overpriced jar of age-defying moisturizer or feel furtive when I sidle up to the makeup counter and catch myself experiencing what society calls vanity? Anne Lamott comfortably lives in this gray area—in her book, *Grace (Eventually): Thoughts on Faith,* she decides, "It's only when you think you need to be concealed, because you're unacceptable, that makeup causes harm."

Through my loving eyes, my friends are beauties every one of them, all ages, shapes, sizes, and colors. We all deal with conflicted body image "stuff" in different ways. One diets, though I don't think she needs it, and that's okay. Another will spend hundreds of dollars buying what she calls "hope in a bottle" to hide the demon dark circles beneath her eyes, and that's okay, too. One is saving up as though for college for a series of hair removal treatments. Another is heavily into the all-natural lifestyle, but still shaves her armpits and legs—a hairy dilemma.

As far as my own body, ladies, the news is not good. Gravity continues its southerly pull. The little age spot formerly hidden under the arm of my eyeglasses is now big enough to require its own zip code. My natural hair color now includes swaths of solid white around my face, like an old dog.

The deadline I had given myself to stop coloring my hair has come and gone—I've pushed it back another decade.

My greatest obsession has become my hands. Genetics gave me a propensity to moles, age spots, and hand crinkles. Looking at just my face, you might peg me for 40 (no sneering, please), but if you were to see me hand-modeling, you might guess 70. The most recent horror was when a friend glanced down at my hands then exclaimed in distress, "Karen, they're so crepey, you need to put some lotion on!"—and I already had. As I have always said, the sting is not that it's not okay to have signs of aging at "the appropriate age," but that having those signs *now*, which is *never* the appropriate age, is NOT okay in my book.

In some ways, thank goodness, I've become less self-conscious about my body as I've become older and wiser. But it's really a case of two steps forward and one step back. It helps if you can laugh, like at the commercials for Nivea anticellulite lotion targeting what appear to be women in their 20s. 20s?! Honey, they don't know from cellulite!

Going to the gym surrounded by mirrors is a nightmare—whose bright idea is that? "Yeah, that'll bring the overweight and sedentary folks in for sure, a chance to look at themselves grunting in unflattering positions reflected all over the room!" Even in the women-only gyms, which you'd think would know better. Yet we've always been surrounded by mirrors, haven't we, like the mirrors of our own self-judgment, mirrors of celebrities sporting heroin-chic gauntness and stylist-assisted perfection, the mirror of others' eyes, whether a mother or a lover.

An inspiring woman I met recently put a new twist on the Ugly Duckling metaphor, as she told of her lifelong struggle with weight and how she finally came to love herself as the swan she is. She radiates self-confidence; now, she says loudly and sassily, "You see me as a swan because I tell you I'm a swan!"

Maybe it really is true what Anne Lamott says: "Joy is the best makeup. Joy, and good lighting."

Where Are All the Good Men?

Where are all the (good, single) men? No, really, where are they?

I've got women friends out there doing affirmations, working the Law of Attraction, and practicing wishful thinking. I have friends who are 12-stepping their way to meeting a mate. I've got friends who are searching for men online, in singles groups, at church, at work, abroad. We're reading *If the Buddha Dated, Casting Your Net*, and *Calling in the One*.

Of course, it doesn't help that we live in an area where there are more single straight women than single straight men, especially as you get older. The problem is that men our age (whatever "our age" happens to be) often seek women 10 or 20 years younger than they are. This royally screws up the already unkind demographics of singledom. At some point during many a night out with the girls, someone only half jokingly remarks how much easier it would be if we were lesbians, because we all know so many great single women.

So who is out there, anyway? Never-married guys—intriguing but suspect. Divorced guys with children—but you have to really understand that their priority in these years is their kids, it's not going to be you, and if their priority isn't their kids, are they someone you can really respect anyway? Separated guys—I'm off guys who are spewing venom about their soon-to-be exes, yet it's an urban legend that that is the time when you have to snatch up these guys, because they remarry or repartner very quickly. I have a friend who in some settings doesn't mention she has a child until she knows a guy a while. (On the other hand, there are the single-parent groups, where it's all right out there—yup, you've got serious baggage!). Players—who's got time for that nonsense? Widowers—very big shoes to fill.

We have to talk about online dating because almost everyone these days knows at least one couple who has gotten together that way. I have friends hunched over their computers nightly on OkCupid, PlentyofFish, Match, and JDate. (My favorite cautionary tale was when a friend was contacted on the site by a man who turned out to be the husband of one of her best friends!) I know one woman who went into online dating like it was a full-time job, going on multiple dates a week—where did she get the energy? Well, turns out, she couldn't sustain it; after several months, it had come to naught, and she was exhausted. And can we talk about how many married guys are doing online dating and personal ads? Eeeuw.

The guys online are to a one looking for slim, fit women—usually slimmer and fitter than they themselves. Though one 50-something match I received put a picture of himself with huge biceps at the gym lifting weights (I bet he's one of those embarrassingly loud grunters)—what kind of woman responds to a picture like that? And why do I keep getting matched with guys whose number one activity and passion is exercising and keeping fit? Not that those aren't healthy goals, but as number one? An Asian friend finds herself creepily being sought after by guys who like the stereotype of an exotic, submissive woman—which she is not.

I have friends who are currently recycling men they knew from the past, romantically or otherwise. I'm beginning to think that's not a bad strategy, so I've been Googling men from my past so I know where to find them if and when I'm ready to dip my toes back in the old boyfriend pool. And a few have even looked me up (Classmates.com and Facebook are good for this.). One friend has for the past year been happily in a relationship with a man she knew years ago, once a neighbor, now half a continent away. They're flying back and forth, but what's going to happen when they run out of frequent flyer miles?

One year I held an Un-Valentine's party for my single women friends, complete with sage burning and magic spells and potions and (of course) delicious desserts. Amidst those casting spells for a new mate or burning talismans to mourn an old one, one attendee was having trouble deciding between two men (and we tried not to hate her). She was the woman who still had tons of guy friends, most of whom were secretly or not so secretly in love with her. But—she hadn't met her mate either.

None of us spends our days crying into our lattes about not having a man, but there are certain occasions, certain times of the day (like when you lie down in bed at night), that your mind and your heart goes to that place that wishes for a warm body, someone with whom to bid the day—good or bad—farewell.

We are wise enough that we don't need or expect a man to complete us; we do not believe that we are somehow less for the lack. We continue on our path doing what we do while subscribing to various philosophies: 1) that you can't look proactively for a man, just do what you normally do and you'll find one by accident, or the variation on this, my personal favorite, "stop looking and you'll find him" (which is actually how I met my ex-husband, but that's another story); 2) that if you're not with someone it means you haven't learned the cosmic lessons or become the person you're meant to be yet and thus aren't at the right point to receive the right man even if you meet him; 3) [insert name of last failed relationship] wasn't the one for you.

Is it that we have to be 100% whole in ourselves before we can meet the right partner? Or does becoming so whole thus make us too much for many men?

Is the distressing disconnect demographic, or just plain demonic?

How to Look Good Naked

Despite showing horrible movies that cast women as victims (albeit ultimately triumphant), Lifetime TV does a good job with its original series. An effort some years back, "How to Look Good Naked," was the bravest show on TV. I watched its first season hoping as many viewers found it as powerful as I did. They must have, because Season Two grew to hour-long episodes. In each, host Carson Kressley, fashion guru of the late "Queer Eye for the Straight Guy," takes one woman, or sometimes a mother and daughter or sisters, through a voyage of self-discovery of their own body. It is not exploitative but nurturing and revelatory.

The goal is to "turn body loathing into body loving." Not with lipo, teeth whitening, diets, nose jobs. Not with the better-fitted clothing or new hairdo that are part of the show but incidental to it. It's about reclaiming what one woman refers to herself in her 20s as: "that bold, beautiful girl who loved her body."

Refreshingly, the show is not about making over our bodies but about making over our body image. Carson calls it "a perception revolution," and I really don't think he exaggerates with that word "revolution." The women learning to feel good naked come in all shapes and sizes, with all manner of hyper-critical body image issues and media messages about what makes a woman acceptable, never mind beautiful. This show bares it all, cellulite, back fat, the whole magilla. Early in the show comes the brave part—stripping down to underwear and facing oneself in a full-length mirror, with Kressley and camera crew present. This has so much humiliation potential, but we do not feel exploitation or tackiness, only caring.

In one typical episode, a woman is initially in tears, saying she can't believe she's become "one of those people" who can't love her body. Her body issues keep her from the dancing she loves. She uses wild clothes to protect herself. Through a series of exercises Carson teaches her and viewers to "stop focusing on *changing* the package but start focusing on *embracing* the package."

One of the fundamentals of the show is that women do not see their own or other women's bodies clearly. To help women gain a more accurate perception of themselves, he creates experiences like bringing them into a room with a half dozen or so women of all sizes, standing in a line. He then asks the woman with him to look at those women, lined up roughly by size, at the part of them that she thinks is the biggest on her, and put herself in the line where she thinks she fits. In all these exercises the result is that the woman has misjudged her own size and thinks she is bigger than she really is. The woman who started out one episode crying doesn't even recognize a picture of her own body Kressley shows her with some others for comment. She likes everything about that body when removed from the mirror of her own self-judgment.

Each woman's journey ends with a nude photo shoot. Tasteful, with a sheet or sarong, and glamorous, not titillating. It's a bold finish representing Kressley's mantra: each of us should look in the mirror, "and say it's OK to be who you are. I don't want you to hide. Hiding sucks." You go, Kressley!

A new book landed on my desk as I was thinking about "How to Look Good Naked." In the foreword to *About Face: Women Write about What They See When They Look in the Mirror*, edited by Anne Burt and Christine Baker Kline, makeup artist Bobbi Brown reminds us what we're up against. On her 18th birthday, her mother offered to buy her a nose job, saying it would make her more beautiful. She turned it down then and reminds us now, "A mirror can and should be a tool that empowers you, not an instrument of oppression."

Watching an episode, I sat in my recliner with my right leg cut wide open just a week after knee replacement surgery. It was swollen grotesquely and the bruising was vivid. Who would have expected that to me the "beautiful" legs I aspire to would be when the right one heals and I have matching thin vertical scars over each knee symbolizing my restored strength and mobility? It's a different way to look good naked. As Kressley says, "It's called confidence and it looks good on everybody."

Anatomy of a Sleepless Night

Close book, set the alarm, turn off the reading lights. Get comfortable, prepare to drift off.

Realize it's been more than a while and I have not drifted off yet. Swear I'm not going to check the clock but I do. It's been 45 minutes.

Get up and pee. Careful not to turn any lights on so as not to send wakeful cues to my brain, per books and articles I've been reading on insomnia and need for good "sleep hygiene."

Lie back down. Sure I'll go to sleep now.

Trying to remember the name of fabric store my mom used to take me to when I was in elementary school. Wonder if my heavy emphasis on *old* memories these days isn't healthy, if I need to make some *new* ones. Think about how to do that.

Mind jumps to how much last night's TV season premiere of "Rescue Me" sucked.

Intermittently worry about the implications of not getting enough sleep tonight.

Consider turning the alarm off now and skipping water yoga in the morning, but it's the last class till late summer. Stay strong, keep hands off the alarm.

Alternatively consider telling friend I'm too tired to go to outdoor concert and dinner the next day but afraid of becoming an unreliable friend. So scratch that.

Suddenly realize I must try and get an old friend from high school onto Facebook. He's on Classmates and I can always email him through that, but that's so static.

Ponder how Classmates ever stays alive in the marketplace.

First click on the light thinking I'll read for a while, then instead get up and work in my home office for about 40 minutes. After sending off a number of broadcast emails, realize 3 a.m. may not be my finest hour for carefully crafted prose sensitive to client needs, or mindful of not offending boss. Prepare to deal with possible fallout the next day.

Stop in bathroom to pee again before rolling back into bed.

Think of future blog topics, then worry if I don't write them down I'll forget them. (Of course I will. I just remembered something I started to make a note to myself about four hours ago, and between the time I thought of it and moments later when I pulled pen and paper out, forgot.) But don't want to turn on light so make a few notes in the dark, hopeful they'll be legible in the morning.

Run through mental "to-do" list for next couple of workdays.

Think about where I'd like to have dinner with a friend over the weekend.

Wonder if I feel like braving the crowds later in the week at the new location for fireworks. Hate new location, miss being able to watch them from across the lake in my own neighborhood. Worry about my increasing hermit tendencies and I do so love fireworks and have missed them for several years now.

Wonder how many actual hermits there are in the world. Mind wanders to caves in the forest of unspecified Asian country where I imagine long-bearded men and old crones who come out only to make sage pronouncements.

Idly wonder how I will ever get a book proposal done if I spend my free time and creative energy blogging instead, but feel I am forced to blog by today's marketplace and agent expectations.

Think about how to make my blog posts shorter, but if I do it'll take longer to do my notification emails than the blog itself. Decide to get up and check on how FeedBlitz or other service can help me get rid of need to manually do the notifications. Pull foot back in bed before it hits the floor, sure that going back on computer at 4 a.m. will not aid sleep efforts.

Remember and write down in dark reminder about a thank-you note I need to write and gift certificate I have to buy to enclose. Wonder what recipient's favorite restaurant is.

Consider getting up to pee again but realize I really don't need to, I'm just bored.

Alarm goes off. Summon all my willpower and do not hit snooze alarm. Resolve to try and go to bed early tonight. Hah, like that'll happen.

Camp Complains-a-Lot

Earlier this year when asked to recall memories of sending my son to camp, I was amazed at the floodgate of memories that opened and washed right over that more recent time, flowing all the way back to my own childhood experiences of camp.

I went to Camp Featherfin, which I liked fine, except for the fact it was outdoors and there were bugs and dirt. My main memory was setting up the camp fire and making goulash that was pretty tasty. Campers went swimming in Lake Winthrop (even when not in camp I took swim lessons there in the early morning in what felt like sub-zero temperatures). As an adult I learned the lake had been contaminated with dioxin. No point even beginning to ponder the implications of that for me or the thousands of kids and adults who spent their summers in those waters!

I also remember when I was around eight years old, in one of my many young volunteer activities as apprentice to my uber-volunteer mom, packing lunches for a camp for underprivileged kids. The most fun part was that the Hostess factory from a few towns over-delivered packages of Hostess CupCakes to my house in big metal racks, stacks and stacks of them in our carport—not for me, for the campers, but still there was something heady about it.

I did go to sleep-away camp on my own one time, and all I remember is how much I hated it and complained about it. I never was big at going outside my comfort zone, physically at least, and that included having to put up with a scary environment over which I had no control, and kids who saw an insecure, unathletic, braces- and glasses-wearing girl who was developing early as prime bullying material. I sent frantic postcards and letters home but was unable to convince my parents to come and take me home.

Let's see, other heartwarming camping memories…How about getting lost in the woods at night at a Girl Scout sleep-away camp (my mom was a troop leader) next to some kind of huge detention center/jail, which I discovered finally arriving at a barbed wire fence? Or idealistically heading to New

Hampshire one summer to be a camp counselor for troubled inner city youth, and freaking out, whether unable to hack the pressure or homesick or both, I'm not sure, and bailing out?

Of course, camp is not what camp used to be. If I was looking at camps now I could study newspaper writing or website design or yoga or learn Italian. I could stay in an air-conditioned cabin in the mountains, or on the beach in a yurt. My delicate tush need never touch the rocky, buggy ground, I need never stumble in the scary dark to an outhouse, and my food need never come with pine needles in it. For that matter, I could have stayed home. But then where would I have learned to make goulash, macramé a friendship bracelet, or sing "Row, Row, Row Your Boat" in rounds?

More Vamping about Camping

Writing my last post about going to day camp and sleep-away camp also got me thinking more broadly about camping. When I was a kid that was the main thing we did on summer vacations, despite my desperate dislike of bugs, outdoor toilets, and getting my hands (much less my body) dirty. Though I complained at the time, I have a rosy glow of memories of a stream of summers driving in gorgeous New England mountains, swims in lakes in New Hampshire and Maine, and picking blueberries at our campsites to go into my mom's pancakes made on the propane stove. Meals camping also included Hickory Farms beefstick, a summer sausage my mom would fry up instead of bacon with eggs for breakfast, instead of bologna for lunch, and, well, I'm sure we had it for dinner, too, in lieu of something!

Perhaps the most Norman Rockwell camping trip was in 1969, when my dad and mom and younger brother and I sat amidst dozens of other families one night at our campground watching on a small TV screen as men walked on the moon for the first time. It was fitting that we were not isolated, each family in our own home, but out there under the stars, from all over the country, in community.

One of my last family camping memories, dragged along at 14 or 15, was to Fundy National Park in New Brunswick, Canada. There was a gorgeous park with a huge bowl of grassy lawn where I hung out with other similarly parentally-inconvenienced teenagers. I developed a huge crush on a long-haired, guitar-playing, soulful older boy (I've always been a sucker for musicians) and created an elaborate fantasy of how we could see each other after summer was gone, since he, too, lived in Massachusetts. Of course he was completely clueless and of course I never saw him again, but decades later I'm still unable to hear Crosby, Stills, Nash & Young do "Love the One You're With" without thinking of him.

When was the last time I went camping, anyway? Perhaps it was in Taiwan in my early 20s. I traveled with a friend, Judy Chen, from Taipei down to central Taiwan where she had friends in college. We hiked around some beautiful scenery, but the most amazing thing about that trip was the amount of food my fellow campers carried and the feasts they prepared just on campfires.

I didn't take my son camping when he was growing up, though I gave him opportunities to do so with others. He wasn't a fan, though he has become very outdoorsy as a young man. Good for him. But he accepts the fact that as far as his mother goes, the closest I get to camping is staying in a motel instead of a hotel. Because I'm just not a happy camper.

Friends and Family

Mothers Telling the Truth

"I believe that mothers should tell the truth, even—no, especially—when the truth is difficult."

—Ayelet Waldman

Telling the truth about motherhood and encouraging others to do the same has been a theme in my writing and in my conversations with other women since I became a mom 25 years ago. Because I firmly believe that if we do not, we are doing ourselves and our children a huge disservice.

Believing that we are perfect sets us up for huge downfalls, for the universe never lets us get away with that kind of self-deception forever. Pretending that we are perfect, making others feel small and inadequate as mothers by letting them see only what we want them to see, the shiny side of our mothering without the dark side, hurts everyone ultimately. It perpetuates harmful stereotypes and unrealistic parenting expectations, and it prevents us from getting help when we need it—whether that is in the form of actual assistance or simple compassion.

First, some truth-telling from this writer mom—I suffered from postpartum depression (PPD). To be more accurate, it began as prenatal depression and it just kept on going. At some point I'll share more about what PPD is like, but in short, it is an abyss from which you don't have the resources to believe you will ever climb out. When I had it, the medical profession barely recognized it, and obstetricians and pediatricians had little response to a numbed mother's attempts to let them know something was very wrong.

I was, I suppose, a high-functioning post-partum depressive. I took very good care of my baby, and no one could tell that I was dying inside. And I had just enough gumption in me to reach out, first to find an organization called Depression After Delivery (a rare source of information that also put moms suffering in touch with moms who'd come through PPD), second to call a pioneering therapist who ran an ad in a local parenting newsletter in the Dallas area for a new moms' support group, and third, upon finding that the therapist herself was on maternity leave, to call up one of the moms in the group.

Bless that therapist, Ann L. Dunnewold, Ph.D. And bless that mom, Cathy, who picked up the phone, heard a stranger in despair, immediately put her infant in her mini-van and drove to my house and picked me and my son up and took us out to meet with her informal PPD playgroup. They brought me into the fold of that group and to the compassion, professional support, and medication I needed, all of which brought me back to life. Quite simply, they rescued me.

Years after the postpartum depression was gone, I continued to muddle along as an imperfect parent, though, and continue to be one to this day. I have made mistakes. I have made lots of mistakes. I could have done so many things better. I cringe at some of the stupid or impatient or less-than-compassionate things I may have said or done over the years not only in direct interaction with my son, but in interactions with others in his presence. I wish I had pushed on some things I didn't, and that I hadn't on some things I did. But my son had a great childhood and has grown up to be a wonderful young man. And I was a good-enough mother. We are, most of us, good-enough moms. And that is not a put-down. It is life, in all its glorious imperfection.

I call out the moms who share with one another only the stuff about being a mom that feels safe, and feels politically correct. I call out the self-righteous moms who want to tell other moms that their way is the only way to mother, whether it's a grandmother who thinks the way she parented her child is the way that child should parent her own children, or a breast-feeding fanatic who doesn't allow for the fact that in some cases a woman has to make the choice to bottle-feed and that's okay. Because what's right for us isn't always right for someone else. And while it may take a village to raise a child, that doesn't mean the village can run roughshod over a woman who is doing her best—her imperfect best, which, truth be told, is all any of us do as parents.

I am not, obviously, talking about cases of physical or psychological abuse, about criminals. I am talking about the rest of us—who sometimes snap and yell at our kids, who only after a botched talk with a child acting out remember the training or advice on how that could have gone down better. Whose houses are full of dust bunnies, sometimes or always. Who find ourselves in an argument reduced to the child's level, whining and cajoling, where we've totally lost control of the conversation or lost sight of the fact that we are the parent and they are the child. Who forget it's our turn to bring snacks to t-ball and have to run to the closest convenience store and grab something last minute. Who have never been room mother because we can barely keep it together working a full time job and taking care of the kids and maintaining some bare minimum level of housework. Who when alone in our house with our baby with our husband working late again and at our wit's end with exhaustion, have locked ourselves alone in a closet and screamed so the baby wouldn't hear us and be traumatized and the neighbors wouldn't report us to child services.

The rest of us, who the best Mother's Day present, some years, might just be, if we admitted it, to have our partner take our beloved child out for the day and leave Mom alone for the whole day. Who don't shop only the advised perimeter of the grocery store, where the produce and other healthiest foods are, but steer our carts through aisle after aisle of prepared foods, tossing "helper" this and "mac" that into the basket with wild abandon. Who have let loose a string of curses a trucker would be proud of when our computers have gone on the fritz, or the dog crapped on the carpet, or the bottle of orange juice slipped from our hands. Who have fought with their child's father in front of them even though we swore we'd never fight in front of the kids.

For about five years I wrote annual articles in *Washington Parent* magazine called "New Year's Resolutions for Not-So-Perfect Parents," some of which were picked up by other parenting publications around the country. Since then I have continued to remind mom readers that there's no such thing as supermom, that they have to take care of themselves in order to take care of their kids, that they should trust their own instincts, and that there are other moms out there floundering and learning on the job just like them. Because that's the truth.

I'm Turning into My Mother!

Okay, now it's official—I am turning into my mother! On a recent airplane trip not only did I put all the liquids in my carry-on into the required quart-sized Ziploc, I decided to carry my other toiletries in two other plastic bags. In my defense, I was moving my purse contents hurriedly into a laptop case, which had no dividers for small items. Even as I did it I could remember recoiling in horror when my mother used to reach into her purse and—in public!—pull things out of the plastic bags she carried regularly, so much so that I bought her a set of attractive cosmetic bags she could use instead. Sigh. (I haven't seen them since.)

My relationship with my mother has never been black-and-white. I don't know about you, but I've got separation issues. Being close is a double-edged sword, I think, for girls and their mothers. All the years I was growing up, Mom was prominent in our small town civically and socially. Townspeople were always calling me by her name and telling me I looked just like her, which I found unnerving.

As an adolescent I could not understand why my friends tolerated or even invited her presence, when I wanted to crawl under a rock rather than be seen in public with her. Yet she was always helping young people who were in trouble. Now I've tried to do that for my son's friends, too. She was also the one who dragged me to a meeting of a new teen group, which ended up becoming a wonderful group of friends. Don't you just hate it when your mother's right?

What I then saw as overpowering, now I also see as being a good role model. Ultimately it was some of both, I guess. I certainly learned about volunteerism and civic responsibility from her. Finding my way in high school after rocky middle school years, I finally broke away from her sphere. Then, after college, moving hundreds of miles away really did the trick. As Alix Kates Shulman puts it, "Those ties had once been so tight that to honor them, or even acknowledge them, was to risk being hobbled by them. Only after I had made my own way in a world that excluded her did they begin to seem benign."

Flash forward 20 years and Mom moved down here to *my* town, and started going to the church of *my* newfound faith and in *my* neighborhood, studying at our local community college with the same undergraduate major *I* once had. I had an instant resurgence of the push-pull emotions of my childhood, of feeling in her orbit, once again. My bristling defensiveness was magnified by the fact that I had my own child by then. We had very different ideas about parenting—hers, typical of her generation, involved playpens and schedules and discipline—mine, well, not. Now, as my son has flown the coop for college, I understand what it is to feel no less fierce love and protectiveness for an adult child as for a tot, and have compassion for Mom's own demonstrations of that.

My son, Sammy, knows that the single most effective way to push my buttons is to compare me with his Nana. Like when I was flipping the remote one day as we sat before the TV and I tried to stop on the "Meerkat Manor" show on Animal Planet, which my mom watches for hours at a time. He teased me mercilessly.

Like Mom's, my hair has thinned so that I now sunburn on my scalp. But I refuse (so far) to wear a hat every time I go out, partly because of my own personal sense of style, partly because Mom does that. Shall I admit that sometimes now, when people are still saying I look like her, I can actually see the resemblance? I also inherited my, shall we say, buxomness and weight problems from her, though I try not to hold that against her.

Recently I have been known to phone her or someone else I care about to let them know about something special on TV I think they'd enjoy, though I roll my eyes when she does this to me. I still have a visceral spasm of distancing once and a while—like when I had to use a cane before and after knee surgery last year, and hurried to give it up so I would not seem like Mom, who used one regularly. Mother and daughter matching props, that was just too much, and hey, I'm 28 years younger than her!

All the defenses against turning into my mother that I have spent an adolescent and adult lifetime building are crumbling with age—hers or mine, I cannot say. I am grateful that I inherited her strength and resilience, so perhaps one day I, too, will be a tough old broad. Thanks, Mom.

Gifts and Being Known

Several years back, my son and I went to pick up my mother to go out and celebrate my birthday. She had been very mysterious when we talked that morning, asking that I park close to the front door and Sammy come up to her apartment. When they emerged from her building, Sammy was carrying gift bags that were clearly heavy, piquing my interest. When it came time to open the many wrapped bundles inside, the first tissue paper parted to reveal—a rock. I'm sure people around us at the restaurant were puzzled. But I knew. She had heard me months before half joking, half griping about not needing more tchotchkes to clutter up my home, but needing rocks to hardscape my tiny front patio. Since then my nearly 80-year-old mother, who no longer drove, had been collecting big, beautiful smooth river rocks for me, as she went about her daily routine, walking back from a nearby grocery and spying one in the grass, or in a taxi driving through a wooded area (and I think she may have committed a petty larceny or two from a sidewalk median strip). She painstakingly put them in her little shopping cart she pushed everywhere and schlepped them back to her apartment. I unwrapped more than a dozen rocks that day, with the certain knowledge that my mother *got* me.

The gifts that blow us away are not necessarily the most expensive or the fanciest. What distinguishes them is that they give us a sense of being known, at a deep level, by the gift giver. It's also really cool when someone sees something in you that you don't even realize, like giving a gift of a piece of clothing you would never have thought would look good on you but that suits you perfectly, or some music you wouldn't have chosen for yourself but ends up stirring your soul.

You might buy something for a loved one's collection, unconsciously hoping that it will bring a smile to their face and that maybe, every time they see or use it, they will think of you. When I have opened over the years birthday and Christmas gifts from one couple—a lavish hand-beaded necklace in spectacular shades of purple, a lushly soft lavender throw, funky fine crafts. Sure I love the gifts in the concrete, but even more in the abstract. I am known. When I carefully choose one friend a cookbook, she knows that I know her (though she's recently cut me off as she is trying to scale down her 300+ collection).

A knowing gift can be a nice surprise from someone (and let's admit it, often that someone is a man) who is clueless about gift-giving. My grown niece's stepfather recently bought her a stuffed sea turtle for her birthday. "It was the best thing ever," she pondered, touched. "You'd never think he would ever think of that."

One Christmas I opened a gift that would have baffled anyone but giver and giftee—a plastic bag full of tea leaves, a scrap of paper with instructions, a compact fluorescent bulb, and a can of sweetened condensed milk. But this friend and I always ended up at a Thai place when we went out to eat together, and I invariably remarked as I ordered one how much I loved Thai iced tea and wondered what kind of tea they used to give it that orangey color. And we had recently seen the film "An Inconvenient Truth" together and vowed to do more in our daily lives to save the environment.

Gift-giving can be taken too far, of course, and *not* giving can mean being known, too. I used to spend way too much money on gifts. I realized a number of years back that just because I saw something that would be "perfect for" so-and-so didn't mean I had to buy it for them and that overspending was not honoring our friendship or familial love. My gift list is shorter now, and with friends farther out geographically or whom I haven't seen for years, we have just ceased gift-giving in unspoken agreement. Even many closer friends and I have agreed not to give gifts some years, or to make a shared experience (a cultural event perhaps, or a spa trip), rather than a thing, our gift to each other. When the economy's been bad there's been less gift giving and gifts have been less costly.

Two of my friends have a tradition for birthdays of bringing over any kind of food you want and any movie for a party "in." One year they brought me my favorite Moroccan food, but what I remember was the absolute feeling of love that came with their gifts. One brought me a stick wrapped in a gorgeous silk scarf—a wand with which to make three birthday wishes—and a simple bamboo chime. She didn't know when she bought it that I actually collected chimes and gongs; she just knew that the sound would soothe me. The other friend brought a white ceramic lotus leaf that she could not have known was the twin of one I had recently admired in a shop in Charlottesville, but didn't buy because I was trying to "be good."

Maybe that's what the real excitement of Santa is for kids even, not just getting fun stuff, but the being known part—Santa knowing just what you wanted. Sure, sometimes it was from a list or a whispered wish in the ear when you sat on his lap, but even then—wow, he *got* you!

As one friend put it at her birthday party, "It's just wonderful when people get you. That's the best."

Parenting in the Gray Areas

Is there any experience that more embodies the concept of gray areas than being a mother? It's all about paradoxes, push-pull and give-take. It's about always loving your child so much you think your heart will beat out of your chest, about sometimes wanting to strangle them, about the delicate balance of giving them roots and wings, dependence and independence, them pushing your buttons on one hand while tugging on your heartstrings on the other, keeping them safe but letting them grow, wanting to give them more and better than you had but not wanting to spoil them…

Nothing is simple; there is judgment call after judgment call; they come fast and furious, expected and unexpected, and you just pray each time that you've made the right choice.

Order and chaos are two of the opposites in parenting. You might be striving for the former, but you'd better have a high tolerance for the latter.

A big issue as a parent, one some people pretend we're not supposed to think about, good martyrs that we are, is balancing our own lives with those of our kids—self-care. In theory, I've always known that I can't be a good parent to my son unless certain of my own needs (creativity, friendships, relaxation) are being met. In practice, I need to be reminded of that once in a while, even as I constantly remind my friends who are moms. When I was living in China about 19 years ago, I was struggling on a number of levels, and berating myself for not being perfect at helping my son adapt, too. A Canadian mom buddy brought me a plate of chocolate chip cookies and said, "Karen, it's like they say on the airlines when they're doing the 'in case of emergency' drill. 'Parents, put your oxygen masks on first and then put on your child's.'"

Another tricky area with parenting is "do as I say, not as I do." When Sammy was nine he filched a pen from the waitress at the diner where we had breakfast, and when I said something, he replied, "Well, you do it." And I said, "Just from hotel rooms, that's different." Uh-huh. So you have to do the best you can with modeling ethical behavior, and 'fess up when you mess up and they call you on it.

Togetherness and apartness teeter on the scales, too. Barbara Sher wrote, "If you don't learn how to respect your children's 'otherness,' if you get too involved in their private time, their games, their schoolwork, their friends, they won't know how to stop defending themselves from your potential interruption, even after they're fully grown." This could account for the overly defensive posture I take with my loving mother as an adult, but that's another story. I have bent over backward to stay on top of and involved with my child's activities while giving him lots of space. Or to put it in a fishing metaphor (why, I don't know, since I don't fish), you've got to give them some line but know when to reel it in. Now that he's in college, I tread lightly too, remembering with chagrin my own mom having had an uncanny sense of timing, calling when I was in the midst of partying or doing something during which I *so* didn't want to hear from my mother.

It's hard not to occasionally get your own childhood mixed up in your guidance and observations of your child's. My son was always popular at school, which I continue to awe at because he seemed to have the complete opposite experience as me with middle school, where I felt like an outcast. He makes fun of my having been a hippie and became the opposite there too, from his preppy clothes to joining a fraternity. I felt guilty when he said he hadn't joined one earlier because he knew how I felt about them. When he did join, he assured me, "Don't worry Mom, it's one of the nice ones, but the cool one."

In those matters on which we do believe in black and white, no shades of gray, we'd better be sure to at least offer up both. We have a universal moral obligation to educate our children about the inequalities and injustices in the world in which we live. How can we do this without giving our children an overwhelming sense of doom, of sadness? Quite simply, we also offer them faith and hope and evidence of our and others' actions against injustice.

There is often a sense of the ground shifting beneath your feet as you parent over the years. Just as you think you're getting it down, another earthquake, another phase.

Parenting—it's the mother of all gray areas. But ah, the grace. Ah, the grace.

Unconditional

I am blessed with an inordinate number of very wise friends, with whom I can not only goof off and have fun but also with whom I can talk about things that really matter.

One such friend and I were catching up. A lot of crap was going down for both of us, most traumatically her dad's being diagnosed with a life-threatening disease. She told me about visiting her parents, about going to the doctor with them, about her mother's fear of a future without her husband. And then she said she was just so, so glad that she had been able to get through all the wildly opposing views she and her parents held, and all the anger and all the resentment—and get to a place where she and her father were reconciled. "And I suddenly realized that *they* are *my people*," she said, "the people that would do absolutely anything in the world, in a minute, for me."

That got us going on our changing relationships with our parents. Yes, indeed, they are our people. Our parents are irreplaceable. They would go to any lengths to help us. And now, we had to be our parents' people, too.

I tried to pinpoint what had happened with my relationship with my mother in recent years. I spent decades focusing all my efforts on separating my identity from my mother's. But what in God's name would I be doing now still trying to separate at my age and hers? I appreciate all that is wonderful about her, and am willing to name those traits I've inherited from her—well, the positive ones, at least! Also, with age my mom has shrunk a few inches, and maybe that physical reality somehow is a metaphor for no longer feeling she looms over me.

I was finally able to extend to her the compassion that I had been working on extending to other people. And when that happened, everything shifted. It opened up an empathy about our identities as mothers, as single women, as human beings on journeys of aging. I love the time we spend together.

So there's that. There's also a sense both my friend and I have that our parents have softened with age. We debated whether this happened because for the first time they have a sense of vulnerability (or is it just the first time we realize it?), or because they have a strength in their own identity, a being comfortable in their own skin, where they don't have to prove themselves to anybody.

She and I also talked about the great circle of life from being a child to being a parent yourself. Now *we* were the ones who would do absolutely anything for our own children, no matter what they did, or what they said, or how much they took us for granted, just like we did our own parents for so many years.

A couple of years ago the defensiveness with which I'd related to my mother for so many years was staring me in the face in the form of my son's suddenly irritated dealings with me. Wow, I did not see that coming! I realized I didn't want that outdated relationship with my mom to be the model I presented for him to relate to me. So I started back-pedaling for all I was worth, and trying to explain to him the transformation.

Another friend used to have her own issues with her mother. But in a short few years she has gone from a standoff to inviting her mother to live with her, and doing that with a genuinely open embrace and respect that has her mother retaining her dignity even as she has to recognize her increasing dependence.

And yet, while in some ways the tables have turned, our parents continue to be "our people." A recent trip to visit my father was an immensely nurturing experience, thanks to both him and my stepmom, largely because I left all my problems behind and didn't have to make a single decision or be in charge of a single thing for those few days.

Then, just a few days after my return, it was Christmas. My mom had always been very anxious about the careful handling of her mother's delicate, gold-rimmed china, which had been stored at my house for years. That anxiety made *me* anxious and not inclined to use it for many years. But recently I've been getting it out at holidays, because I know how much it means to her. After a delicious dinner, we sat relaxing over coffee and dessert. I told everyone to leave their dishes on the table, saying since Sammy cooked, I'd clean up and wash them by hand as usual later. My mother raised her head deliberately, looked at me as though proffering a dare, and said, "Or, we could fly in the face of common wisdom and put them in the dishwasher." She was more worried about me (nursing a couple of physical ailments at the time) than about the possibility of a slight wearing down of the gold on the dishes she cherished. And that, for me, was golden.

"Our primary relationship is really with ourselves. Our relationships with other people constantly reflect exactly where we are in the process."

—Shakti Gawain

Stroke of Luck

"Show me the way to go home, I'm tired and I want to go to bed..." My mom heard someone singing in the hallway and chimed in on the subsequent verses, whereupon a delightful red-headed Irish woman came into her room and the two of them finished the song (one of my mom's mother's favorites) together in fine fettle, then chatted happily for a while longer.

That was three weeks ago. My mother had been in the hospital for a week after suffering a stroke.

We were lucky in so many ways. My niece in Massachusetts, up unusually early for a Saturday, had called her grandmother to say hello. With both nursing and EMT training under her belt, when my mother started talking, Alyssa immediately realized something was wrong. She told her to hang up and called the state police to have them get in touch with 911 down here. She then called me. And I, barely beginning to wake up, decided not to answer and to just call her back in a bit. Seeing her name on my phone's screen again several minutes later and even my sleepy brain realized I'd better pick up. As I threw on my clothes and passed a toothbrush haphazardly across my teeth, my mom was already hurtling toward the emergency room in an ambulance. At this point all I knew was what Alyssa had told me, which was that Mom was having trouble speaking and breathing.

At the ER, I hurried back to my mom's curtain. She was conscious and undergoing tests. As I arrived the doctor told us both what I had feared: she had had a stroke. My heart fell, and then I numbed myself sufficiently to go into medical advocate/pillar of strength mode. My brother—my only sibling—lives in Massachusetts, which felt like a million miles away.

As the hours rolled on, the doctor asked my mom if she'd ever been told she had a heart condition. Except for a minor murmur, the answer was no. But she did—her heart was in atrial fibrillation, meaning her heart was not pumping efficiently and this could allow blood to pool and clot. It's likely this is what caused the stroke, which could have happened much earlier even than the phone conversation I'd had with my mother the night before, when nothing unusual caught my attention.

When I'd arrived, my mom had been slightly slurring her speech but was understandable, at least by me. One side of her face was drooping ever so slightly. As the day progressed, though, she became less easily comprehensible, resorting to writing things down on a pad of paper to communicate, thankfully having not been paralyzed from the neck down at all by the stroke. But by nightfall, even the writing failed her and she had become unable to make herself understood. We were both terrified.

Amazingly, during a hurried conversation out in the hall later, the doctor said her speech might improve. I couldn't believe it; I thought once you lost it, you lost it.

What followed was a largely nightmarish stay for my mom in the hospital, shuttled to four different rooms, with what seems to me to be the systemic problems of hospitals, not enough nurses and techs, so patients are left frustrated and fearful, waiting, waiting, waiting.

Did I mention that my mom had just two weeks before the stroke finally been discharged from all of the physical and occupational therapy and wound care needed after a fall that broke her hip in December, and subsequent complications? The poor woman who has been out only once, aside from ambulance rides and doctors' appointments, for Mother's Day, just days before the stroke, since November!

The days were a blur of good news/bad news. The day she was admitted the medical staff was anxiously trying to figure out how long ago she had had the stroke, so they could administer the magic bullet of tPA (a protein that could break down blood clots), which had to be given within five hours. As the clock ticked on, that soon became a secondary point as they conferred with her and her regular doctor and learned that the next line of defense against another stroke on the wave of the first, the anticoagulant warfarin (Coumadin), was counterindicated for my mom. She had had a severe gastric bleed a number of years back and was at risk for more bleeds, including in her heart or brain.

The good news was that the second morning as I was walking from the parking lot into the hospital, I got a phone call—astonishingly, from Mom, whom I'd left the night before speaking gibberish, now slowly able to make me understand what she was saying. My wonderful mother had already had a session of speech therapy early that morning and had been practicing constantly ever since. Not for the first time I felt blessed at her strength. Her speech and her brain power improved day by day, a miracle of the human body and human determination. We were lucky, lucky, lucky.

I kept vigil at her bedside for four days and evenings, trying to help be her advocate (which sometimes meant as little as going down the hall to explain to the staff the urgency of a request for a bed pan, to as much as going to the hospital's medical library and getting the saintly librarian to help me with research on what was happening to her and what to do next). I experienced the frustration and fear with her as her environment continued to spin out of control (feeling a lack of control being something none of us is comfortable with but which very much does not agree with my mom). I made and received a whirlwind of calls, especially to and from my brother and niece (the latter now rightfully anointed as having saved my mother's life), updating them and concerned friends and family from Massachusetts to California.

My brother came down five days in and gave me a much-needed break from the stress of staying 12 hours a day at the hospital. We both felt hopeless at the doctors' inability to decide about whether it was riskier to give my mom the needed anticoagulants (which could expose her to a chance of a bleed, including to her brain or heart, from a minor bump into something or even a heavy sneeze) or not to give them to her (which kept her, particularly with the atrial fibrillation, at a high risk for another stroke). At one point they were trying to push the decision back on us, for which we felt completely unqualified and told them emphatically so. Finally, after more than a week, they decided to give her the warfarin. It's something she'll have to be on and be monitored for for the rest of her life, and she'll have to carefully monitor her eating for her vitamin K intake, too.

Mom's in rehab now, just a few minutes from my apartment. She changed from the place she'd gone for her post-hip-surgery rehab not because she didn't like it but because she was "desperate for a change of scenery." It's been overall a good experience so far as she continues her speech therapy in particular, loving her homework of crossword puzzles and word games and some exercises that seem hauntingly like taking the SAT day after day. She's doing very well with them except for the occasional one that reminds her that her brain power still isn't back to 100%, and she doesn't let that get her down. When I come to visit we often play rousing games of Upwords (her favorite board game, a variation on Scrabble). I've beat her the last two games, but only by a few points. We agree this counts as homework, too. I was there today and she was delighted that her new physical therapist was working her really hard, and Mom asked for more.

I have been under a lot of stress these past few weeks as all this unfolded. My stomach has been in knots, and I've been on what I call the "oh, shit, my mom just had a stroke" diet, realizing it is time to get serious about my own health. I have developed an obsessive relationship with Purell. I've been exhausted being the dutiful daughter, and am humbled knowing that so many more women (and men) out there have been caregivers at a much more intensive level and for much longer. I don't know how they do it.

Mom, as usual, I don't know how you've gotten through all this with the strength and good spirits you've somehow held onto. Yes, growing old isn't for sissies. But once again you are an inspiration.

Our Stuff

Spring Cleaning

What we should really throw out in spring cleaning is everything that doesn't fit—physically or otherwise; things we've grown out of—physically or psychologically; excess baggage, especially that without wheels that does not propel us happily forward; perfectionism (including aspirations to the perfectly organized home); second guessing; should-haves and shouldn't haves; other people's expectations; and self-doubts rattling around our brain closet.

Enough with the lofty metaphors. Instead I've decided to, er, come clean about what we're really grappling with. Back in our mothers' and grandmothers' days, spring cleaning was really about cleaning. Now, look out, people—it's Our Stuff.

Here are just a few of the things I probably should clear out but I can't: An exquisite, vintage black lace dress that was my nana's and then my mother's and wouldn't have fit me even when I was a lithe young woman. Boxes of books I have paid movers to move a dozen times over the years. Various braces, compression hose, crutches, and occupational therapy gizmos I trip over in the basement—remnants of one knee replacement surgery I can't ditch because someday soon I'll be getting another.

The aqua mermaid-shaped candle someone gave me for my foyer bathroom, which boasts a few tasteful mermaid crafts. The candle is borderline tacky (some would argue it's over the line), but it's unique, c'mon! Empty tea canisters—they're pretty and I pay a premium to buy them over cardboard boxes, so I'm keeping 'em! Remnants of a prolonged bunny-collecting phase I went through when my son Sammy was a baby—like the wall thermometer ceramic with the cute bunny jumping over the moon—the actual thermometer is long-since broken, and I don't think you can even buy mercury thermometers anymore, so what am I supposed to do? Why, I'm saving it for that future day when I take up crafting mosaics, at which time I will smash the ceramic holder to colorful pieces and create a decorative tabletop or mirror.

I'm staring at not one but two huge, fully loaded spinnable Rolodexes with contacts from jobs dating back about 25 years (people used to say I gave good Rolodex). What are the chances even 10% of those people are where they used to be or, if they are, have the same phone number? And the info on these cards preceded email! Hmm, if I save them long enough, Rolodexes will become antiques, won't they?

I still have many books from my son's childhood. I'm saving these for my future grandchild. As for antique books I have collected since my own childhood, I plan to read these when I retire. Hah! That's my story and I'm sticking to it.

Lest you think me a hoarder, here are just a few of the things I have bravely tossed recently. A pair of opaque cream-colored pantyhose circa 1985. Several ill-fitting bras. Some uncomfortable shoes. With each charity truck pick-up I have parted with at least one thing given to me but ill-suited to me and not re-giftable. Kitchen gadgets never or rarely used have gone out by the dozens, along with clothes we no longer wear. Skin care products I am now scared to wear after visiting the Environmental Working Group's "Skin Deep" Cosmetic Safety Database. Even though some of them were really expensive.

I've made some progress on the huge box of old—but still working, I swear—telephones, caller ID boxes, USB cords, phone cords, handsets, and earphones, which has been taking up valuable home office closet space for far too many years. But there are a few I just can't let go of. After all, "I might need them someday."

When I recently had a flat tire changed, I was surprised to find a festive tote bag in the spare tire well with gear that I used to carry to the swim center—judging from the 2001 receipt in the bag, well, those toiletries probably aren't good anymore! I tossed the contents but am throwing the bag in the wash, because after all, who knows when you might need a tote bag (and the other 10 you have might be otherwise occupied)?

Things that are definitely going—soon: a commemorative book of the US Constitution, about the size of a briefcase, which I think I got my ex-husband on the occasion of his becoming a naturalized citizen 24 years ago. We've been divorced for 15 years. If he doesn't want it, Friends of the Library gets it for resale!

Honey Nut Cheerios that may or may not date back to my son's last year of high school (he's long since graduated from college now). On the rare occasions he eats breakfast here he doesn't eat cereal any more. And I don't eat this brand. But the sell-by date on the box isn't for another month or so, so why not hang on to it—"just in case"?

Leftover candy from Christmas. (Okay, Halloween too!)

One of my two sets of flannel sheets. Now, though my bedroom can get chilly, I do just fine with a combination of cotton sheets, a blanket, and a comforter, with a little kick of the furnace thrown in. But the flannels go with my bedroom décor so nicely. And what if global warming were to reverse itself suddenly? Or—can't argue with this—what if I lost power one night?

Admit it, you've got stuff you know you should part with but just can't. I don't know about you, but all it takes to motivate me to a spurt of decluttering is watching a couple of episodes of those home interiors TV shows where a crew goes into a family's home and finds GASP!! such piles of junk all over every surface of the house that they can't even walk through their living rooms, cook in their kitchens, or sleep in their bedrooms. Cautionary tales, indeed.

Here are some phrases, no doubt familiar to you, that are the Sworn Enemies of Spring Cleaning. "Just in case." "I might need it someday" and its cousin, "I just know that the minute I throw it away I'm going to need it." "It's one of a kind." "[Insert name] gave it to me," and its even-harder-to-defeat "my [insert name of relative] gave it to me before [he/she] died." "But it was free!" "I'm saving them for my grandchildren" (and the offender's kid isn't even in high school yet). "[So and so] carried it back for me all the way from [insert exotic, faraway vacation destination]." "It's a collectible." And the mother of all Foes of Decluttering—"It was my mother's."

I called my mom just now to confirm the origin of the black lace dress I mentioned above. She was elated to be reminded that I had it and she excitedly told me "the story" of the dress, from being a floor-length formal on petite Nana when she and Grandpa went to Masonic Lodge/Eastern Star dances, to being a tea-length dress on my taller mother for a magical dinner with a young man who thought she looked "like the cat's meow" in it. And that is why some things just weren't meant to be thrown out in the spring cleaning: but I suppose, should I ever part with the dress, that I have something even better now—the story.

Saving the Good Stuff

You may laugh at the stereotypical 1950s "housewives" (and the occasional grandmother still today) who covered their sofas in plastic so they would stay pristine. But aren't we all just as silly about our "good" stuff? Who doesn't have a "good" dress, "good" dishes, "good" earrings we rarely take out and enjoy?

For Christmas dinner I took out my nana's china, painstakingly stored in padded zipper containers, tucked into a cabinet in my front hall whose only reason for being there is to hold that china since my mom's place doesn't have room. Mom was so touched to see it when she arrived, and reminisced about how she had eaten off that china since she was a toddler. Despite the fact it has to be hand-washed and -dried and is such a fuss, I've vowed to bring it out more often.

I work from home, but as fond as I am of PJs, I know I have to get dressed occasionally. If I'm just going to be hunched over my computer all day, I toss on sweats whose pants have shrunk to flood length, perhaps with a misshapen velour top. I'm always saving my beautiful clothes for when I'm going out. What the heck am I waiting for? I have enough "good" sweaters (by which I mean non-shrunken, non-pilling, non-figure-defect-highlighting) I could wear a different one every day for weeks. I wear loose granny underwear and old bras losing their elastic on a day-to-day basis and save the lacy spandex confections, for—when? A hot date with Liam Neeson?

For many women, the "saving the best for later" credo accounts for clothes in the closet with tags on them a year or two after their purchase.

I have tried to be better about this. I decided a few years ago that I had so much gorgeous hand-crafted costume jewelry, I wanted to see it instead of having most of it tucked away in drawers. I bought a little wood tie rack and hung it on my bedroom wall to display my necklaces. They are art, and seeing art in my personal space pleases me. I also drape some of my scarves willy-nilly across furniture so I can see them more often.

On a visit to a spa in Bali, I purchased a pretty bottle of massage oil with a tiny scroll attached to its neck. I keep it on a shelf in my bathroom to remind me of that paradise, but was always saving it for a special occasion. Now it's been 17 years and I'm afraid to open it and find it rancid. Talk about a message in a bottle!

Using the good stuff more often would let us enjoy its provenance more—remembering the pleasures of the place we got it, or the first time we used it.

I have certain books that I save for later too. I always keep an unread humor book for travel: I'm a nervous flyer and this is a good distraction, as though a good laugh will forestall turbulence or wind shear or pilot error. I keep some unread spiritual reading tucked away for when I'm in a dark place and need some soul-lifting.

Another common item we hold back on is scissors. Every house, doesn't it, has a couple of pairs of dull-bladed cutters we use, until what, a special scrapbooking competition, a magazine article by an author we really like? Get out those good scissors with the sharp blades! Or turn the others into good ones again, sharpen them, replace them!

Sometimes we call things "good" for who knows what reason. What, do they have an evil twin?

My friend Dana as a little girl had an Easy Bake oven and saved the cake mixes for some special occasion. By the time she went to use them, the mixes were hard and inedible. She thinks she still holds off on using things because she's "satisfied now and might need more later."

There's another perverse spin on this, too, the "it's too good" rationale. Dana and her partner gave her grandmother a wonderful electric fry pan—and she put it on a doily in the dining room and never used it. "It's too good" tends to be the province of elders, although it can sometimes be code for "what do I need some crazy complicated gadget for when what I have works perfectly well?" or just plain "I don't like it."

After my recovery from knee surgery, I finally got to put the throw rugs back down. The braided rug in the living room has one side sun-faded, dog-lounging-faded, the once-black sections now charcoal at best, worn from years of treading on it with great love. The other side is just as it was when I bought it, very vivid black and yellow stars and periwinkle patterns. Without hesitation I laid it out faded side up. I'd save the good side for company.

Truth be told, a lot of our things perish tangibly or intangibly before they get much use. Just what is it we're all saving the "good" stuff for if not every precious day of our lives? Let's remember that *we, now* are good enough for the good stuff.

Hide and Seek in Our Handbags

Women are the butt of endless jokes about all the stuff they carry in their purses. But whom do you turn to when you're out and about and cut your finger and need a bandage? Certainly not a man. Where are you going to find a ChapStick when your lips get dry on a cold winter day? Not a man's wallet, that's for sure.

In addition to our handiness, the contents of our purses and our wallets reveal a great deal about us. Sort of an archaeological dig without the dirt (unless you count those lint-covered mints that have been on the bottom for a year). I got some Washington women to empty their bags and "spill" to help me demonstrate.

While there is a strong movement among most women I know toward decluttering, this does not include their handbags. This isn't just "stuff," it's "important stuff" that we identify as such by our willingness to haul it around day after day, weighing us down as we walk, wearing grooves in our shoulders, taking up space on the table at the restaurant (or setting on goodness knows what kind of germs on the floor), tangling up in the packages we carry in from the car, bumping into people on a crowded bus.

Some items turn up regardless of who the woman is or where she lives. The driver's license and credit cards. The cell phone and/or iPad. Kleenex. Nail file and/or fingernail clippers. Lipstick, gloss, or balm. A dead giveaway she lives in the DC area is the federal ID on a neck cord, though other clues are harder to follow—like that Sally's purse also holds a large brooch she was wearing recently on her coat, but had to remove it because it set off the alarm at security as she entered her agency's building.

The keychain often has its mysteries, too. There's that key we've been carrying for as long as we can remember, but what exactly is it to? Not home, office, or auto, then what? Safe deposit box? Place we used to live? Elderly parent? Ex-boyfriend? We almost all have items in our purse that don't belong there anymore. A good friend found a defunct Curves gym membership card (she quit a year ago), and better still, a key card for the parking garage for a job she had left 10 years ago.

Most handbags include a makeup holder, and everyone has their own preferred container as well as their own version of "the essentials." We of the dry skin carry hand cream and face cream; they of the oily skin carry face powder or blotting papers. Some of us prefer a see-through case to help us find what we need; others like to hide their beauty secrets.

Health information often lurks inside our purses, and not just in co-pay receipts. The contact wearer has solution, the glass wearer a cleaning cloth. One friend has a child's physician referral and diagnosis slip as she prepares to switch doctors. The plastic card from my orthopedic surgeon attests to knee replacements being the reason I always set off alarms at airport security. One woman is easily identifiable as lactose intolerant; another's stressful job shows in her jumbo containers of Advil, Excedrin,and Pepcid. Many of us find pills in our purses, sans bottle or box—what one friend calls those "free-flowing tablets of medicine"—and wonder what they are and what they're for. Another not-uncommon item is the report for a recent clean mammogram; carried around sometimes for months, it represents a big relief, an annual affirmation of health or a brush with fate cheated.

You can guess at a woman's age from her purse contents. Generally, the more business cards from medical specialists, the older you are. Someone carrying around a checkbook is probably not Gen Y. For that matter, neither is someone carrying cash. Photos with grandchildren are of course slam dunks on age. And need I add the AARP membership card? New bifocals have turned up in my recently-turned-40 friend's bag. In 27-year-old Alicia's wallet, "the one card that's so worn out you can hardly see it anymore" is her DSW frequent buyer card (she has more than 100 pairs including many ankle-wrenching high heels), whereas I have a laminated Comfort One Shoe Club card.

You can tell the writers and readers. A Kindle bespeaks a literary bent crossed with a love of technology. Despite having a smartphone, I can never be without a pad of paper, and at least four pens (so I have half a chance of being able to find one at any given moment) and a highlighter (so if I'm reading a book I own in some downtime I can highlight passages I like). Two friends carry Post-its, though as one says, "Don't ask me why, I have no idea." Readers always have their library cards with them.

You can tell what's going on in the world around us by what's in a purse's deep, dark interior. Hand sanitizer? Scary flu pandemic. Movie rental and grocery receipts for higher-than-usual amounts of junk food—and road salt? Impending snowstorm. Goodwill receipts? Bad economy. Cell phone photo of a loved one in uniform in a foreign setting? We're still at war. Our information-overload society is also reflected inside our satchels. We keep little cards hidden in our wallets with our bank account numbers and slips of paper with the instructions on how to remotely access our office email. And witness the number of people carrying around half a dozen partially used Metro cards, or duplicates of frequent buyer cards we couldn't seem to find the original of so now have four stamps on one, two on the other.

A little-discussed fact is how discreet a carrying case for snacks a purse is. Alicia kept a Cadbury Turkish Delight candy bar in her bag "in case of an emergency— like getting stuck in traffic" (Before, alas, the candy bar was discontinued.) I used to keep Snickers, but now it's Special K bars. Our tastes and schedules can also be determined from grocery lists, receipts for fast food we claim we don't eat or a credit card receipt reminding us of the indulgence of an expensive meal at a favorite restaurant. Is there a frequent buyer award card in your wallet for a great little Vietnamese pho place or the Pie Gourmet? A call-ahead card for your favorite restaurant? Tattered newspaper review of a new dim sum joint you've been meaning to try? (OK, there's the age thing again—young women don't have tattered newspaper reviews, they just have iPhone apps!) I laughed longest at the list in one friend's purse with names like From the Tank and Killer Juice—boxed wines she had researched online; she laughed, too, and said, "I guess what that says about me is that I drink wine in quantity."

I believe that romantic status can be intuited by the presence or absence of breath enhancers in the purse. A single friend, Ellen, explains as she catalogs her purse contents to me: "Breath mints, because I'm forever hopeful I'll meet a guy I want to kiss."

Of course, certain "delicates" are giveaways of frequent overnights at a regular romantic partner's home.

Hobbies, politics, and passions can sometimes be gleaned. Laura's wallet bulges with receipts from Home Depot for construction materials for the pottery studio she's building in her backyard. My wallet holds clues like my Landmark Bethesda Row discount card (love my indie and foreign films), ticket stub from a recent folk series holiday concert at BlackRock Center for the Arts, and expired (due to finances, not interest) membership to the American Visionary Art Museum. Alicia has about 40 ticket stubs from all the Redskin games she's been to. Sally carries the schedule from her local swim center. Ellen carries her International Campaign for Tibet membership. I proudly sport my American Red Cross Champions for Life card.

Want to know if a woman is a greenie commuter or Beltway warrior? Check the purse! Metro card? Bike lock? Garage parking pass? Half a dozen gas credit cards? Bus schedule? AAA membership? Business card for a limo service? Vanpool phone number?

Whether the subject lives on a champagne or beer budget is easy (Bloomie's and Tiffany receipts vs. Target and Marshalls, discount card for Unique Thrift Store vs. Black American Express). Our bags tell traveler's tales sometimes as well, with stray foreign coins, or flattened souvenir pennies from US tourist destinations. Purses carry our hopes and dreams, too—from promising fortune cookie messages to lottery tickets.

We carry our families around in our handbags with other precious cargo, in the form of things like school carpool schedules and business cards from our adult children. We carry family secrets, too, like one woman's slip of paper with a list of numbers corresponding to TV channels. Her father, in a nursing home with dementia, can't remember the channels on his TV, so she's going to type up for him which numbers to push for the things he likes to watch, like the news.

Most unusual handbag contents in my admittedly unscientific survey? 1) Rolling papers, which one woman picked up on a trip to Costa Rica, not, she insists, for personal use but for a friend; 2) a young friend's diploma, laminated in business card size, from American University; and 3) a small Christmas disco ball.

Alicia once pulled needle-nose pliers out of her purse on an out-of-state trip with her belly dance troupe, and everyone laughed. But she was Jane-on-the-spot when a costume with metallic elements started coming apart. The official motto of former Girl Scouts and all purse-carrying women of the world? "Be prepared!"

Consumer Concerns

I'm suffering from study exhaustion, aren't you? No, I don't mean cracking the books. I mean hearing about studies released by government agencies, by scientific institutes, by medical journals, by activist groups. Is there anything we eat, drink, apply to our bodies that won't give us a disease or kill us or feed injustice?

There are too many competing claims on our hearts and minds as we choose the various tangible tools of our lives, and if you're heeding one set of considerations, there's a pretty good chance you're ignoring or violating another. We're supposed to eat organic, clean with environmentally safe products, throw eco-friendly weddings, buy alternative gifts, shop fair trade, not buy products from countries or US companies with unfair labor practices, and track recalls for kids' toys. I'd barely have room for a lipstick in my purse if I carried around all the guides that help you track the shoulds and shouldn'ts.

I heard from gay friends that a grocery chain discriminates against gay workers, but they are the closest store to me. So should I do the right thing environmentally and save gas but the wrong thing ethically and go there anyway (and just hide the bags from my friends), or do I boycott them but be environmentally unfriendly by driving farther to another grocery store?

We've struggled with good carbs/bad carbs, good fats/bad fats. "They" (just who are "they," anyway?) tell us that popcorn's a good low-calorie snack and it becomes a favorite of many dieters. Then we're told that there's a carcinogen released by the inside of the microwave popping bag. Is it any wonder we throw up our hands? We're afraid to eat meat because of mad cow and E. coli and because we shouldn't eat anything with a face, so we eat more vegetables, but oops! Now there's E. coli in our veggie supply, too.

And what about milk, which we grew up believing was the nectar of the gods? It's good for getting calcium and may help us lose weight; it may be an abomination and we should drink only soy or rice milk instead.

What about all the people who are lactose intolerant without knowing it, and could that be at the root of every physical ailment you've ever had?

Studies show there's more bacteria on our kitchen counters than on our toilets. But we're not supposed to use sponges in the kitchen anymore because of all those studies showing they just push dirt around. Okay, I started using paper towel. But wait, no, now I can't use that, because it's environmentally irresponsible, so it's back to using sponges, but they have to be microwaved to clean them, and what about the electricity use there and the potential-but-never-proved concern some still harbor about microwave safety?

We read in the newspaper every day about another new scourge of infections sweeping the country so we switch to antibacterial sprays and wipes, but now it turns out that a) those are making the bacteria more resistant, and/or b)they don't really do any better a job than soap and water, depending on whose study you're reading.

We're told repeatedly, "drink more water," so we buy and drink bottled water because we can grab it and go and get our mandated eight glasses a day. But now we're told we can't drink bottled water anymore, only tap, which is actually better regulated and safer. Plus we need to feel guilty the plastic bottles, though recyclable, are bad due to their sheer volume. So we go and buy a popular brand of reusable plastic bottle, then lo and behold, we read about some of them leaching hormone-disrupting chemicals into the water. What's a gal to do?

Surely you've heard those stories circulating for years that there may be a link between the aluminum chlorhydrate in deodorant and breast cancer? Debunked or no, the compelling fear of somehow being complicit in our own disease has me periodically trying yet another "natural" deodorant that just doesn't get the job done. So easily swayed am I by the constant barrage of urgings to consume only natural products that last weekend I caught myself almost buying a new "environmental control" deodorant for $19—$19 for a stick of deodorant, am I crazy?!

The occasional nail polish I apply may be toxic, too, it turns out. But the selection of "healthier" ones atop the checkout counter at Whole Foods is woefully small compared to my favorite line with its whimsically named colors. And God only knows what the hair color is doing, but I just can't give it up.

It seems triclosan mixed with chlorinated drinking water can release chloroform. Now do we have to give up the dentist-recommended toothpaste that fights gingivitis—with triclosan?

Fashionistas once laughed at shoes and bags made of "manmade fibers" and flocked to leather, but now we're being told if we love the environment, we'll buy organic vegan shoes instead. We shunned polyester and ran to natural fibers like cotton, but now it turns out growing cotton actually leaves a large environmental footprint.

Even caring for our pets is tricky. We've been admonished by our vets for years not to forget flea and tick meds, but now we're hearing that these may not be good nor may immunizations routinely given pets.

I guess this overload of information and controversy is one of the prices we pay for—or rights afforded us by—a free-speech society, and we should be grateful.

Still, there's no question, it's tough being a consumer these days. In some areas I've made changes, in others I plan to but haven't gotten around to it, in others I'm just not yet willing to. For now, just pretend you don't see me roaming the store aisles, shaking my head and muttering to myself.

Editing my Life

It took two weeks of back-to-back snowstorms, but I finally got around to the monstrous amount of filing that's been looming over me in my home office for, oh, about five years. I'd staved off utter chaos and degradation a couple of times over the past couple of years, once enlisting a friend who was out of work for a while in a filing marathon (that's how you can tell who your real friends are!), once or twice when my son was on school vacation (though I had to twist his arm to get him to work for me, even at more than minimum wage!), and again in a failed attempt to bring on an office assistant to help with my overwhelming workload. But in a couple of days straight, followed by mop-up operations over subsequent weeks, I filed for hours on end, and even more satisfyingly, threw away five bags of trash and recycled about four feet of stacked magazines, folders, travel brochures, and papers. I donated boxes of books to Friends of the Library and I got A Wider Circle to pick up a piece of furniture that would find a place in the new home of a family moving out of a shelter. I purged and organized (mostly the former) like a fiend.

I am sufficiently self-aware that I realized pretty quickly that all this organizing and decluttering was an attempt to impose order on one room while the bigger picture was that my life was spinning out of control. More and more commitments and obligations, some externally imposed but many I will own to having placed on myself. Even the interesting things on my calendar, the theoretically fun upcoming events, the meetings of organizations I find meaningful, were crushing my spirit. There was no space in my days and my nights anymore. I was busy from the moment I rose in the morning until the minute I blessedly fell asleep. Which was another problem—I was having horrible insomnia, the kind where you stumble around all day with sore eyeballs barely able to keep your lids open, the kind where you are in a daze, like someone put glue in your brain. Something had to give.

I woke up one morning last week and somehow these words were right there at the front of my brain: "I just can't keep opening up endless portals into my life, endless claims on my attention." Like most messages I get, I had been hearing this message from the universe for some time, and nodding, and then going right along being "crazy busy."

I realized that for all the editing I was doing in my writing, what I now needed to do was edit my life. So I have been. I've been processing the sheer volume of "stuff" in my life—"stuff" being everything that demands my time and my attention, two commodities that are too precious to waste. I've been practicing discernment about what to keep and what to get rid of in my life just as I was deciding what papers to file and what to shred in my home office. I have withdrawn from the steering committee of an organization I remain committed to in other ways, and may be scaling back some of my writing outlets (among them, some book reviews I've been doing for a national website that has turned my favorite thing in the whole world—reading—into one more thing on my to-do list—*so* not cool!).

I'm also reassessing my connectedness through technology. It is a blessing and a curse, one of the many gray areas I love exploring in life. I'm a big fan of email, but I've just unsubscribed to more than half of the e-newsletters I used to get, and got off of notification lists on "deals." And I'm trying to limit the time on my computer at night, though that's challenging because that's when I do most of my writing. I love Facebook, and I love reconnecting with old pals from my hometown and friends from college, but what does it say if I find a couple of them living in the same area as I do and we want to get together but just never seem to have the time? I worry that I am a tree with roots that are expanding but not deep enough to keep me strong and growing.

I've also been in a period of hypercreativity, but that, too, is a double-edged sword. It keeps my brain churning nonstop, and all the connectivity I'm feeling, like sparks flying and synchronicities firing with new people I'm meeting, whether in person or not, all of that requires follow-up and time, too.

All this decluttering of papers and junk is liberating and empowering. But just as the biggest challenge in filing or tossing is not letting the piles reaccumulate, the biggest thing for me now is figuring out why I commit to or seek to experience more than I can healthily accommodate in my life and how to stay focused on the people and activities that matter. I have to edit the story of my life, day by day. And make space for grace.

"I want to touch you in real time
Not find you on YouTube.
I want to walk next to you in the mountains
Not friend you on Facebook."

—Eve Ensler

Rolling Blackouts

My life just flashed before my eyes.

I'm not sure why I found myself carrying three Rolodex cases downstairs from my home office. I'd been looking at the two old ones across the room from my desk for years and decided I could do a small decluttering/purging project while I watched TV. I didn't realize it was going to be a retrospective of my life.

So, how do you tell when it's time to toss a Rolodex card?

- Rolodex? Are you kidding me?
- The card has a phone number with no area code on it. Because you didn't have to dial area codes for local calls (remember?)
- The person on the card has died, or you think they might have but you're not sure.
- It has information on your student loan. Not your kid's, yours.
- It's for a divine little French restaurant in Georgetown. From the days of expense account lunches. RIP (the expense account lunches, not the restaurant).
- It's a no-longer-in-service phone number for an old grad school classmate you last saw when she told you she'd gotten a job at "The State Department" (you have to picture the air quotes) and promptly went incognito, never to be found again.
- It's the number for the guy you went on your first date with after your divorce. Well, you thought it was a date; he thought it was just coffee.
- It's for your master's thesis advisor. Whose specialty was the Cold War. (Remember the Cold War? Me neither.) And he's been dead for years.
- It's for Compaq Tech support. And it's been a decade at least since you've owned a Compaq. (Are they even in business still?)

- It's for the new cupcake place that opened in town. Back when you still thought (why?) it was worth three bucks for a cupcake, and still thought it was a good idea for you to eat cupcakes.
- It's for the airport shuttle, and quotes the price as $19 (it's now more than $30) and says your child (now 25) could ride free.
- It's for a manicurist you used to see in your old office building, back when you could afford the time or money for a weekly manicure.
- It's for a favorite store that shut down, a victim of the economic downturn.
- It's a list of hours various Northern Virginia public libraries are open. And you haven't lived in Northern Virginia since the 1980s.
- It's from a telecommunications industry job you used to hold, and is one of a half-dozen cards you have for Ma Bell companies. You know, Illinois Bell, Southern Bell, all those Bells that haven't rung for about 20 years since the monopoly got broken up, after which all the vigorous competition among the new telecom companies brought us lower prices and great service, right?
- Likewise, a card with the number for your own phone company, C&P Telephone.
- It's for a grocery delivery business, about 20 years pre-Peapod.
- In the Doctors section of Rolodex cards, cards not only dating back to the OB/GYN who delivered your (now 25-year-old) baby, but back to the student health center at your university.
- It's the name and address of the nice couple with a house in the country who adopted your dog when you had to give her up before moving into a condo after you got married.
- It lists all the bookstores you frequent(ed). Including Common Concerns, The Globe, Crown Books, Mystery Books, may they rest in peace.

- It's for the airlines you used most. And the list includes Eastern Airlines and Braniff.
- It's the home phone for the wonderful college intern you had in one of your trade association VP positions. And he now owns his own company and lives in China.
- It's got the number for a dog walker and dog trainer for a doggie you haven't had for years.

Someday I'm sure I'm going to be going through the same process in my Gmail contact list. For now, history in a box of Rolodex cards has transitioned mostly to history in the "cloud." I hope my memories, my history, will be safe there.

Cataloging a Changing Way of Life

I just got a blast from the past. Cleaning out some files, I came across an article I'd written nine years ago called "Catalog Come-ons, or How I Got into Mail Order Mischief," about my addiction to catalog shopping. I'd never gotten it published but took a look again today to see if I could update it and recycle it somehow. Not a chance, I quickly realized. Wow, nine years was like a lifetime ago. First and foremost, catalogs? Really? All of my references were hopelessly dated in the face of today's online shopping opportunities. Second, I'm just not the consummate consumer I was back then. A lot of water under the bridge financially, and radical reprioritization of my income (little realities like college tuition, and what unfortunately was a novel concept to me for years—savings). Plus as I get older I'm more about simplifying and decluttering rather than acquiring. Third, there were many references to my then-husband. Fourth, they're just not sustainable environmentally.

Still, there was a time… I used to be an inveterate shopper on foot, so of course I segued nicely when direct mail catalogs really took off in the boom years for boomer incomes. In the beginning, it was just catalogs for clothes and shoes. (Not that I ever bought shoes from a catalog—who can do that? Not this size 11 wide!) Then, the catalog companies got a bead on me and the floodgates opened. New, more exciting catalogs started coming my way. Stuff. Neat stuff. Beautiful stuff. Handy stuff. Exquisite stuff. Stuff I could really use for my kitchen/yard/living room/son's room/bathroom, stuff I never knew about but now I couldn't do without. Stuff in just the right color, in just the right size, just the right height, just the right fabric—how did they know me so well? (Ah, how naïve I was.)

Let's face it—catalogs were and are entertainment, not just convenience. I used to read the old Banana Republic catalog cover to cover. This was back in the day when Banana Republic was about safari and adventure wear, not what the young urbanite is wearing to work like it is today. It wasn't that I was planning a trip to Kenya and needed supplies, but because I was an armchair traveler, and it had that special aura of good travel literature. The Vermont Country Store catalog has, well, everything you can think of, from tried-and-true skincare remedies to flannel nightgowns to discontinued candies you used to eat when you were a kid.

Certain catalogs are fun to read because they're written so cleverly. I've more than once thought that writing copy for catalogs would be a blast. (I was so jealous when Elaine on Seinfeld was writing for the J. Peterman catalog—which, by the way, I just Googled, and they're still in business, and the descriptions are still positively poetic!) Other catalogs make their impact with stunning photography. Still others, like the National Geographic Travel catalog, are about big dreams. As Anne Fadiman wrote in her book *Ex Libris*, "My problem..." is that I never want the item, I want the associated fantasy."

I cruised catalogs for the one-of-a-kind (hey, never mind that they have 6,000 in the warehouse) items that suited my style. I laugh when I think of the crap I didn't buy (most of the crap I did is long gone to yard sales and donations). Flower pots with bread-baking kits in them. (I don't even bake!) I was also an easy touch for humor, hence the near-order of a T-shirt that read: Baroque (adj.): When you are out of Monet," and the address labels with the picture of two nuns, one asking the other, "So, what are you wearing tomorrow?"

Coldwater Creek still gets me, I love their clothes, their service, the whole nine yards, but I've been meaning to call and cancel the few other clothing catalogs I still get. Well, maybe I have to keep Soft Surroundings, too. True to its name it's full of rich textures, clothes you want to wear (snuggly cashmere sweaters, angora socks, embroidered caftans evoking Mediterranean nights), linens to sink into (floral quilts from Provence I just admire; an aqua bamboo blanket I did buy and is so soft and warm), and powders you want to brush gently across your cheek. Everything is sensual, tactile. I love the beauty of even the descriptions of the colors, like the silk pillowcases in blush, celadon, bisque, lake, or champagne and the silk velvet poet's shirt in garnet, peacock, chocolate, or azure. What can I say? I'm a color junkie.

Mail order, whether catalogs or now websites, have taken some of the fun out of being a collector. No longer are collectibles things you found here and there, surprises in dark corners of antique stores or on a vacation somewhere exotic. Now if you collect foxes, lighthouses, teacups, or piano-related items, they not only all have their own catalog, they're likely to have 10 websites. After a while, the thrill is gone.

I have, of course, taken my waning shopping libido online. Although I will say, there's one thing you can't do with an image on a computer screen—take it to the mirror with you to be sure a particular color of a sweater pictured in the teeny tiny photo will go with your hair and complexion. And flipping through a catalog is such a good complement to mindless TV watching when you just haven't got enough brainpower to turn off the box and read a real book instead.

I used to deal with the onslaught of frequent and numerous catalogs by pitching them directly into the trash can without so much as cracking them open—there, I just saved $45,677.95 plus shipping and handling! Of course, eventually we all learned there was actually a way to stop all those catalogs coming except ones you specifically requested. And now I have a fool-proof system for lingering catalog longing. I go through the dwindling number I still get, circle favorites, and carefully fold down the pages for items that catch my eye. When I reach the last page, I go back through and carefully weigh the choices, unfolding the pages of some I decide I can't afford or can live without. Then I put the catalog into a beautiful antique, woven Chinese wedding basket where it lives until several months later, when I open the basket up, pull all the accumulated catalogs out, and toss them in my recycling bin, without spending a penny.

Much of my catalog and later online shopping was with gifts in mind, but I have also cut way back on excessive gifting with friends and family, as we've all realized we don't need more stuff and instead focus on shared time together, as well as donations to charitable organizations in lieu of holiday and birthday gifts.

Yes, once upon a time I could tramp through malls for hours, giddy with the phrase of the day, "shop 'til you drop." Well, drop I did—financially, that is, and finally realized that my endless consumerism was not compatible with living responsibly, nor was it feeding my hungry soul. Now the malls no longer beckon, and the catalogs have lost their siren's seduction. I lost my lust for shopping. It's the end of an era. Now connecting to others and to the universe draws me in instead, and creativity is a bigger come-on. Oh happy day!

Confessions of an Anti-Domestic Goddess

I am the first to admit, I am a fan of shortcuts, cheats, faking it, prepackaged, and prepared. Now I have met my cosmic twin, and she is Lisa Quinn. I'm referring to our philosophies on housekeeping—the less the better, the simpler the better. Quinn is a writer, TV host, and "recovering Martha Stewart junkie" (we part company there as I've always thought of Martha as the devil incarnate). She's the author of the book *Life's Too Short to Fold Fitted Sheets: Your Ultimate Guide to Domestic Liberation.*

I knew I'd found a kindred spirit when I reviewed the list of chapters in the table of contents: "The Lackadaisical Lifestyle," "Not-So-Good Housekeeping," "Slacker Chic," and "The Half-Assed Hostess." *Paisan*! One of the basic tenets of our shared philosophy is that you must never buy stuff that has to be ironed or hand-washed (whether it's clothing or china or linens). Seriously, is this a good use of your time?

She and I have matching brown thumbs—she kills plants, too, though I may exceed her in this regard. Every time I receive a plant from someone that isn't made of silk my eyebrows hit the ceiling in alarm—have these people met me? Some hardier greenery may hold on a few months but most succumb much more quickly. I've conducted funerals for more orchids, ferns, violets, palms, and other household plants than most families have for goldfish and hamsters.

I long ago decided that if I waited to entertain until my home was perfectly clean, perfectly tidy, perfectly anything, I would never have anyone over at all. So I tidy the necessary surfaces, invite friends for potluck, and throw open the door for a relaxed wonderful evening.

Quinn's hilarious rants combine with tips that will make your domestic life easier (like "17 Meals from a Deli Chicken" and "Interior Finishes That Hide Most Dirt"—news you can use!). One of her most brilliant ideas is to bag the book club. "Who's got time for a book club?" she argues. Instead just invite your girlfriends over for a magazine club, reading from your favorite "rags." Perfect, right? You still get the sharing of ideas over a few bottles of wine, but without all that prep time. (And after all, the glass of wine is more than half the equation, isn't it?)

I was recently reminded of how, shall we say, progressive, my views of housekeeping truly are when I had to interview a cleaning company. The owner asked me for my pet peeves in a cleaning service and I told her how the company doing my home now could never seem to make my bed the way I like it. I gave her a quick demonstration of the way I do like it. She then demonstrated to me how she would make it with a special fold that would make it look "pretty" when you walked into the room. I stopped her halfway through—"Listen," I said. "I live alone. I don't care about a pretty fold in the covers; I care about how it feels. No fold, it makes the covers come up too high when I sleep." Bemused, she agreed to note my preference. Later, she tried to talk to me about what cleaning products she'd recommend between their visits every two weeks. Again, I had to stop her. "I'm going to be brutally honest with you. There are no between cleanings." I can barely keep up with the clutter. I'll wipe the kitchen counter if I've made a mess, or use a disinfectant wipe once in a while, but that's about it.

Thud—that was the sound of my mother keeling over from horror and embarrassment. She bemoaned to me years back, "Oh, Karen, you've really lowered your standards." I prefer to think of it as having raised my standards—for self-care, for giving myself a break, for choosing to give other activities and people higher priority than being a "wife" to my house. And it fits with my strong gravitational pull as I get older and wiser toward comfort over all else. Plus, I am a master at turning what might once have been regarded as "lazy" into, instead, and with a certain self-righteousness, "eco-friendly."

In my never-ending quest for simplicity I recently performed my most bold act yet—I canceled my subscription to *Real Simple* magazine. Good tips, but still too much pressure!

Encounters with Grace

Alive in the Artisphere

Once again my blog is saved from gloom and doom. I was going to write about what a rotten time of it so many of us seem to be having these days, how tough life has become, the grave troubles of the world...So I picked myself up from my navel gazing and went out to remind myself of the beauty that flourishes alongside the blues.

I went to an art opening. Arlington, Virginia is home to the Artisphere, a series of lively multifunction arts spaces in the old Newseum building in Rosslyn. After treating ourselves to dim sum at China Garden, my friend and I rolled across the street to the weekend-long open house. The building was bustling with performances that made my trek to the other side of the river well worth it.

As I browsed one exhibit, I noticed people gravitating to a lobby area. Lemming-like, I joined them, to see across the atrium a group of a half dozen dancers performing on a staircase. I was mesmerized by the beauty of the tightly spaced, measured movements, the elegance of every perfect leg extension, the gauzy skirts over the women's leotards, and the muscles on the male danseurs. I almost wept with the loveliness of it. Bowen McCauley Dance Troupe is stunning. Encore! Encore!

Not long after wrenching myself from my viewing perch after the dancers departed, I roamed into the ballroom to await a performance from Joe Falero and DC Latin Jazz All Stars. Lo and behold, as more people came in and joined me sitting on a bench built into a wall opposite the stage, several of the dancers who'd just performed ended up sitting next to me, so I was able to tell them how much I appreciated their performance.

From the quiet grace of the modern dancers we now spun into the excitement of music that digs inside the audience and stirs the spirit. As the band hit the ground running, a couple moved onto the dance floor who we pegged for pros, perhaps instructors. It was bliss watching them move, the woman a dead ringer for Judith Jamison, a white leotard sharp against her chocolate skin and a bright Caribbean-looking skirt that swung sexily as she did, the man a ham and a half but a skilled one, clearly enjoying himself mightily; their pleasure at each step and swing was infectious. As the musicians hit the high notes with salsa, mambo, bolero, cha-cha, with each number more and more people ventured out to move to the music, until for one salsa there were on the floor parents with babies in their arms, a man in a wheelchair rolling happily around, a woman with a gimme cap and fanny pack setting the floor on fire, a couple obviously freshly graduated from dance lessons, and they all looked awesome. For all of them, and all of us swaying in our seats uncontrollably, it was pure art elevating the spirit.

It didn't matter what anyone was wearing. Dance shoes shared space with loafers, work boots, sandals. Long flowy skirts that moved with lithe bodies shared space with blue jeans on plump bottoms and khakis on scrawny legs. Two little girls, emboldened by their mom dancing happily alone on the floor among all the couples, pranced out onto the floor, grabbed her and danced together. It doesn't matter if you're short, tall, fat, thin, lumpy, sleek, everyone is beautiful when the music infuses you and pulls you up on your feet, and you move under its thrall. Each beat better than the last, bongo, congas, sax, and more, Latin flavor fabulousness—Joe Falero & DC Latin Jazz All Stars, thank you!

I came to heal, and heal I did, heal we all did. On a gorgeous autumn day in an industrial space just over the Key Bridge from Georgetown, in a little urban jungle, we filled our hearts and souls with music, and dance, and life was—life is—good.

Sharing Grace with Sloan Wainwright

A recent folk concert I attended turned out to be more than a great musical experience, rolling instead into one of those wonderful moments of connectedness that linger long after the event. Sloan Wainwright and The Kennedys were playing at BlackRock Center for the Arts as part of the center's coffeehouse series. I haven't been to as many concerts as I'd like in the past year, but wouldn't miss Sloan Wainwright coming into town for anything. This woman could sing the phone book and I'd pay to listen; her rich contralto voice is unlike anyone's and I adore her style. Yes, she's one of *those* Wainwrights, sister to Loudon Wainwright III, aunt to Rufus Wainwright, and so on, but I couldn't give two figs, because with her voice and her songwriting skills she's one of a kind. I also enjoy The Kennedys, this time finding it a particular treat getting to hear Pete Kennedy play the electric sitar, a beautiful instrument.

This concert I was struck by the powerful, affirming lyrics in Sloan's songs, especially on her new album *Upside Down & Under My Heart.* The first glimmering that I'm connecting at a deeper level with her lyrics now, not just her voice, comes as she sings in "Little Bit Right":

> *Everybody's a little bit broken.*
>
> *Everybody's a little divine.*

I got chills. What delicious wordsmithing, what perfect truth!

Her lyrics speak to me in meaningful metaphor:

> *Even when it's all uphill*
>
> *Somehow you find the will*
>
> *To meet the sun halfway*

These are lines in a song she wrote on her album *Life Grows Back* about meeting a 90+-year-old woman in the mountains, but I hear that in challenging times we still need to turn our faces to the sun so we can feel its rays when they come, and that at any time we need to be open to happiness to receive it.

Sloan talks about "All that dwells between the layers of living" as she introduces her song "Between the Lines," and I am gripped by the eponymous refrain:

Between the lines

Is where I'll find

What I am after

The answer lies there

Between the lines

I hear the affirmation that we live and find grace in life's gray areas, between the lines, in the questions, amidst the paradoxes, in all that is unexpected and must be accepted.

During the break between sets I was the first one out to the table in the lobby to buy CDs and had a few minutes alone with Sloan. I told her how I sat straight up in my seat when she riffed between numbers and shared this epiphany in real-time, "I'm becoming very much at one with the gray area, never mind context." I told her about my former "Grace in the Gray Areas" column in *Washington Woman* magazine, now morphed into my blog, and we connected eagerly over this and over the stunning and rare deep lavender jade pendant of the goddess Guan Yin she wore around her neck, the goddess of mercy who also graces my home in two sculptures. Did I mention both our 20-something sons are named Sam? I love a good synchronicity!

A wonderful and unexpected evening, music, a shared gift of grace, and the goddess of mercy—what could be better? Sing on, soul sister!

An Evening with Ram Dass, Krishna Das, and Fierce Grace

No one at the staff meeting that morning seemed to notice. Or perhaps they were just being polite and ignoring the dark circles around my eyes and the fact that I had exchanged showering and putting on makeup for an extra half hour of sleep. How could they know that their colleague had had an extraordinary experience that kept her out late the night before? Or that even when I had laid my head down on the pillow it took me til until 3 a.m. to get to sleep, in no small part due to the rhythmic chants going through my head on a non-stop loop, like when you hear a song on a TV commercial and can't get it out of your brain, only more meaningful?

My friend Laura and I spent all the previous day and evening at Buddhafest, a three-day feast of Buddhist films, music, meditation, and talks. We both needed some spiritual shoring up, and this was definitely the place for that. One of the organizers shared that a man from West Virginia had told him how much the event had meant to him, and how it was a "hope generator." How perfectly that captured our intention in coming and the gift of the event.

As is often the case, memorable events can come where and when least expected. I made a nice connection with a man, Steve, sitting near me when speakers from Shambhala Meditation Center had us break up into twos for an exercise. It was one of those great incidents of synchronicity and recognition where you're both saying, "Wow! We're going through the same kind of experience!"—and it makes you remember you're not alone in this world or in your experience of it.

Laura was chatting with a woman behind us in line, she more intently than I as I popped out to grab another bottle of water and browse the books, CDs, and DVDs for sale tables. I heard that the woman, Lysa, was from Canada and had come here specifically for Buddhafest. I knew that Laura was also talking with her about how much she needed this gathering and its lessons, after a series of events had really beaten her up over the last year and a half. After we sat down, Laura told me what a lovely spirit she had, and how when Laura had asked her of all the retreats and meditation centers she'd been to, which was her favorite, Lysa replied that it was the one she'd created in her own home. Out of the blue in a break between sessions, Lysa came back to our row of seats and knelt urgently at Laura's feet, pressing into her hand a little silver bag. She told Laura she knew how difficult a time she'd been having because she'd gone through some things herself, and that she wanted her to have this talisman. After she stood and disappeared back to her seat, Laura opened the bag to find a gorgeous glass pendant of blues and grays and greens. As she rubbed her fingers over the smooth surface, we sat holding in awe the deeply touching gift, all the more meaningful coming from a stranger.

Although the afternoon's talks and films had focused very tightly on Buddhist meditation and Buddhist lineages of spiritual teachers, it was an evening more in the Hindu milieu that lifted hearts and voices the highest and bodies from our seats.

Krishna Das, the world-acclaimed musician, had us chanting for a few minutes in a call and response before he talked a bit about his relationship with Ram Dass, the great spiritual teacher who came out of the 1960s and reminded us to "Be Here Now." We all knew that Ram Dass had suffered a stroke more than a decade ago that left him partially paralyzed and with speech difficulties. We were all very excited that, after watching a film that had been made of him after his stroke, Ram Dass was going to join us via Skype.

I had already seen the film *Fierce Grace* on Netflix, but it was much more powerful on a large screen in a room full of mindful spiritual seekers and practitioners. Also, on my small living room TV I had not been able to hear Ram Dass in real time from Maui, with the wonderful sound of waves crashing on the shore in the background.

Krishna Das talked with him briefly. Ram Dass said, "I've learned to go within to go in my heart, and certainly my stroke has helped me because it's given me contentment. Here I am, I'm 81 and I'm content!" Later he added, "The stroke was grace. You know, I'm just learning how to inhabit my heart, my spiritual heart. Our guru [Maharaj Ji] gave us love and I'm giving you love, and you will give love to other people, and that's the way it's spent, heart to heart to heart."

One of the audience members asked what we can do to engage the youth of today to look at spiritual teachings and continue to work for peace. Ram Dass replied, "We can be, not do…I tell the youth today, don't get intrigued by information on the outside. Go into your heart because that is where the real information is. Outside is objective. Inside is subjective. Inside is self, your guru, God. All inside of you. Inside of you! When the environment is too much, go inside, go inside," he urged us, then broke into a great big smile and added, "Yeah!"

Ram Dass also told us that we have to embrace change, particularly regarding aging, but that declines in health need not define us. "I am inside," he said, "and I am an infinite being, and then I have this body. The stroke happened to this body, it didn't happen to me. See?"

"It's made it hard to play the cello, and it's made it hard to drive, and it's made it hard to walk," he continued. "But those 'hardnesses' showed me how strong my attachments were." Taking the example of driving, he said that he'd gone from being in the driver's seat to being chauffeured, and he looks at trees and grass now, not the road. "I am a passenger. A perfect passenger!"

We gave a standing ovation and waved farewell to Ram Dass, then settled in for a promised 45 minutes of music from Krishna Das. The kirtan began then, and we had barely chanted one call and response before one after another of the audience members rose to their feet and began to dance, either at their seats or out in the aisles. Small groups of dancers formed and we chanted on and on and on, a mantra, a loud vibration of the universe and praise to God that in this multifaith gathering became praise to the universe, praise to spirit and divine energy, and to living lives of love and peace. The emotion built and the chanting and music from Krishna Das and his band and the audience response grew louder and louder 'til I thought I would lose my voice.

Introducing the film to us, *Fierce Grace* director Mickey Lemle said that one thing he learned from Ram Dass was, "We're simultaneously human and divine, and the trick is to dance in the space between the two, in that tension." And so we danced, and danced, and danced.

Stories on the Train

A day-long train ride lay ahead of me to Charlotte, North Carolina, where I was headed for a visit to an old friend. I was prepared to enjoy lots of quiet time with my books and my journal, and I did, and more. I'm always struck by how cordial everyone is in train travel, smiling, nodding, talking, with an ease absent from the stress-filled world of plane travel. My first encounter reflected that, exchanging pleasantries with the woman next to me in Union Station as she made preparations to board her severely epileptic daughter.

Once on board, I plunked myself down in my assigned seat. Within 15 minutes my seatmate, Linda, and I had had that amazing instant connection and sharing of life stories that women often have, each subsequent layer of revealing changing our initial perceptions of one another. She was safeguarding in the rack above us a huge bag of bagels from Zabar's that she was bringing from her home, New York City, to her children living near Raleigh, where she had grown up. We talked about how we both love trees, about my growing up in Massachusetts, about her idyllic youthful vacations with a lover on Cape Cod. She related how when she decided to leave Raleigh in her early 20s in the late 1960s, she'd gone to stay with her brother who lived in New York. Her parents had hoped he would keep an eye on her, but it was futile. "I had fun!" she laughed. Pink-tipped curls against her chocolate brown face peeked from beneath a purple scarf, a purple pashmina in her lap over black jeans and tee. Her wrist was covered with silver bracelets her former husband got her because, she said, as if it were evident, "he knew I loved silver."

We compared our tastes in books and magazines. She talked about how she was weaning herself off TV, and we discussed needing a quiet space and time in our days to remember who we really are. We companionably offered each other bits of the food we'd brought in our carry-ons for our long rides. Hours later, we were sad to say goodbye, and laughed as she carried so much stuff she had to disembark into the down-South heat wearing her up-North down jacket.

As Linda had slept, snoring quietly, for part of the ride, I enjoyed people-watching. A few bored-looking teens sitting next to their parents listened to iPods and texted. A 'tween helped her considerably shorter mother get several bags down from the rack above with one hand, the other hand and her attention engaged elsewhere, on her cell phone inside her hoodie dispensing advice to a lovelorn girlfriend. A middle-aged woman's elegant attire contrasted with the grocery bag from which she periodically pulled out and knitted a never-ending ugly scarf. A cute 30-something woman earnestly did paperwork, until her craving for chocolate derailed her and sent her to the café car for a bag of M&Ms, after which she never quite got back to work.

A friendly younger man and I chatted as we got off midday at one of the proclaimed smoke/stretch breaks offered. Moving past the cluster of smokers, we basked in the sun and I did yoga stretches on the railings on the platform.

After Linda left, an elderly woman from Wilson, North Carolina sat down. She was visiting family in Charlotte, carrying barbecue in a cooler that seemed heavier than she was. When I asked incredulously if they didn't have barbecue in Charlotte, she replied matter-of-factly, "Yes, but they don't make it like they do in Wilson." (My friend later confirmed this.) We discussed a mutual love of water aerobics and how much we were "not morning people." She was delighted when I shared my decadent mint truffles. We reassured one another when the train was delayed with switch problems and to save fuel the lights were turned off. One of the engineers broke the tension by joking, "I'm going to be lighting candles for you all in a minute here," as he walked through our car.

No cards were exchanged or phone numbers keyed into smartphones, but comforting connections were made among strangers on a train.

Finally disembarking close to 11 p.m., as we walked down ramps from two sides of the platform that merged into one entrance, I saw a young woman with sky blue hair and ringlets around her face and a jaunty black bow, wearing a jazzy black-and-white print blouse with cap sleeves, over a very short, poufy, shimmery beaded black skirt, atop black-and-white fishnets and a pair of chunky, short black boots with heels, their black bows complementing the one atop her head. She was perfect, totally at ease with herself. I entered the station with an ear-to-ear grin.

Seasons

Hope Springs Eternal

Are you feelin' it? C'mon, I know you're feelin' it, too. Everyone's walking around with a bit of a skip in their step and a smile on their face. Work's still stressful, finances still lousy, the world's still full of tragedy and sorrow. What's changed? The sun is out. The air has lost its bitter edge and is seductively warming. Spring has sprung.

Yeah, I know, hopefully I'm not speaking too soon. You can't see me, but I'm knocking on wood. Yes, in the Washington, DC area if you don't like the weather, as they say, just wait five minutes. We may still have some more ups and downs in temperatures, but there is no stopping it. Spring has sprung.

Yes, I'm still dealing with winter's damage, to my holly tree out front and to my vulnerable container plants that had no deep roots in the ground to protect them from winter's ravages. And the damage to my psyche, which is also vulnerable every winter, particularly because of the shorter days and lack of light (my therapeutic Sunbox notwithstanding). I always fall into the trap of globalizing. I think I'm always going to feel this bad and then suddenly the oppressive weight of darkness and cold has lifted. Spring has sprung.

We all awake from hibernation. It becomes more attractive to go out in the daytime for some exercise, to go out in the evening for some socializing. I'm more eager to rise and greet the day. My mom is sprung from her isolation, out cruising around on her walker again, stopping in at her favorite neighborhood shops, no longer having to worry about a rogue patch of ice sending her tumbling to a broken something or other . Outside my window, the geese on the lake are wildly flapping their wings and bobbing under the water, bathing noisily rather than serenely gliding across the lake. Some fowl spring-cleaning ritual perhaps? But I get it! We're all giddy! I feel like flapping my wings, too. Spring has sprung.

The metaphor of spring is so deeply nurturing if we can keep it in mind through the dark days of the year and the dark days of the soul.

No matter what. Reliable beyond reliable. Nothing can stop it. Always, always, spring will come. Enjoy the grace of nature and the never-ending circle of life. Have faith.

June

June is a transition month, like Sunday night is a transition night. The bridge between spring and summer, between merely warm and truly hot, between merely green and lush green. June nights, as they progress, become summer nights; crickets clatter and tree frogs burp. Nights no longer cool as the sun sinks, but stay hot and muggy and wrap themselves around you like a sticky blanket.

For school children, each day in June brings them closer and closer to vacation, to freedom that they appreciate mightily, not knowing how free they really already are just to be in school and not at work. Attention slides, then sinks, 'til teachers give up hope, and school days are filled with recognition assemblies and year-end performances. Goodbye to familiar faces at the desks around you, an element of surprise always around the corner as kids wonder who will sit near them in the autumn. Fond farewells to teachers, mentors. Moms scurrying around buying teacher appreciation gifts. For older students, it's a high-pressure time that threatens to explode them, with exams, final papers, and hearing from colleges or about summer jobs.

Parents half look forward, half dread the prospect of less structure to their children's days. If they are working outside the home, it's a rush to be sure the days are filled with camps. Almost everyone has some kind of vacation to look forward to in the summer ahead, anticipation, even if it's just a weekend trip to the beach.

Those days from childhood of leaving school and flinging oneself into summer stay with us somehow. Even in our workaday world, the air seems a little more full of oxygen, the time binds are a little looser. Summer beckons.

Summer nights, ah, those are a treat unto themselves. I thirstily drink of evening in the summer, no longer bound to my living room by cold fingers of winter and spring evenings, by darkness laying its black blanket on me. Suddenly, summer—light graces us with her presence so much longer (and hurrah for the earlier onset of daylight savings time, too!). Evenings do not look inward, as we huddle together with our closest family indoors, but outward, as extended family and friends join us for barbecues on the deck, as our community shares a concert and fireworks, as all the world comes outdoors to stare into the night sky as darkness finally falls. Neighbors stroll our sidewalks, children's bicycles careen across the corner, lanky teenagers glide by on skateboards. Our eyes follow the path of fireflies flung like stars across the night.

We see each other outside, a spark of recognition, a warm hello, an exchange of news about our day, our kids, the weather. We admire each other's gardens and lawns, perhaps bemoaning the state of our own.

We block off a cul-de-sac to gather together, slapping mosquitoes in the warm night, for a summer block party. We pile the kids into our cars to head for the pool, maybe even, if we're lucky, one who has been away at college, and loiter long after in the parking lots chatting under the bright moon, no cold sending us rushing into our cars but rather the summer night drying our skin, our suits, our hair into kinky mops.

At the beach, the moon draws us back outside long after we are ready to turn in. We gaze at the dark blue-black ocean, and dig our toes into the sand where the cool air coming off the water makes them tingle.

All those extra hours of "up"—of wakefulness, of energy, of light—oh, thank Mother Nature for each long summer night.

June is also a tipping point into a period of time awaited perhaps more than any of the year, made all the more precious because of its fragile finiteness. It's the time to drink in long, long sunlit days, the warmth of the air on skin not burdened by sleeves or jackets, the cool pleasure of gliding through water in a pool or lake warmed by the sun. June days are as long as days ever will be, and heading back in the other direction: it is, in a sense, the beginning of the end.

We want to hang onto pleasures like this, a season like this, but as it always does, the summer will slip away from us. Here we should heed the Buddhists and practice nonattachment, for becoming too attached to a season is folly, sure to end in heartache. And yet even as I soak in the nurturing sun's rays, I am struck sometimes by a fleeting fragrance of bittersweetness, of an inevitable impending loss.

So stride outdoors I will, and splash and bake on beaches, and I will do the back-float while gazing at a perfect blue sky and white clouds passing by, so that I can more gracefully, when the time comes, let go of summer and face the grayer half of the year with something approaching acceptance.

October Night

Magic moon
swollen goddess of the sky
white warm
childish wishes
grownups gazing
Bathing in your light
I am brave
I am calm
I am the wild woman
of the night
Silver and ice
your beams souls entice
Magic moon.

'Tis the Season to Lose All Reason

The holidays are all about misery and obligation. If I didn't have that every year I'd miss it.

—Grace Adler to her mother
on the TV show "Will & Grace"

My default reaction to the realization that the holidays are around the corner for years has been dread. I know it's not just me. For many of us, holidays are classic gray areas, annual occurrences with which we have a raw love-hate relationship.

We spend more time with our families, whether natal or extended, than at likely any other time of year, which is taxing regardless of where your family falls on the dysfunctionality continuum. Time is often compressed because of work and school obligations—how can such a short space of time contain all of our hopes and dreams for a storybook holiday? We trek homeward by plane, train, and automobile, and the usually frenzied trip itself often delivers us to our loving families in a grumpy heap.

Blending our increasingly nontraditional families can be a challenge. We are so far flung now, it's complicated figuring out who goes where for which holiday and how to keep feelings from being hurt when we can't be in two places at once (or two people we love can't be in the same place at the same time, as the case may be). The specters of divorce and death are particularly strongly at the holidays, too. Maybe there just don't seem to be the right number of people at the table anymore, and it can feel more like a time for mourning than celebrating. Me, I mourn not only the breakup of my own marriage 15 years ago but my parents' divorce years earlier. How I envy friends or neighbors who go home to their still-married parents' homes, often still the home they grew up in. My frustration at not being able to provide my son with a Norman Rockwell holiday is combined, I realize, with my continued frustration at not getting one myself.

Staging a holiday meal can be like planning a military campaign, only more political. All that sharing of the responsibility of cooking, even cloaked in convivial conversation, is tricky. For certain family members who shall remain nameless, things have to be done just a very particular way or it's a disaster. And then there's the adage, "if Mama ain't happy, ain't nobody happy," and it's hard for overworked, sweaty Mom, up to her armpit in a turkey's butt, to stay happy while she slaves away and others kick back. Food is such an important part of holiday traditions, which is why families battle over whether the stuffing served at Thanksgiving is the wife's mother's recipe or the husband's aunt's hallowed formulation, or why kids stubbornly rebel if Mom tries to substitute or add a new food into the meal for health or variety or just her own sanity. It's why for years I knocked myself out baking my late nana's sugar cookies and more recently I beat myself up for not having the time or energy to make them.

I do love that Thanksgiving is a truly national holiday not owned by any one religion, available to all Americans (with or without papers), celebrating this difficult but blessed family togetherness. It's a good spiritual practice to sit down as one, say grace from whatever place of faith we hold, and then share what we're thankful for. For those few moments, perhaps, everything shifts into perspective.

Ironically, the Thanksgivings that have been most stress free for me as an adult are the ones that were the least traditional, whether it was bringing Algerian foreign student friends home from college and them teaching my mom and me to make couscous, or when I was in Asia with expat friends cobbling together a traditional meal from the canned goods we'd brought with us, or with the air conditioning blasting in Dallas at a British home eating roast beef and Yorkshire pudding.

More recently, after a series of particularly wretched holiday seasons that left me depressed and my relationships with my relatives prickly, the past few years have improved because, well, I just somehow simultaneously loosened up and took control. Thanksgiving I order some food from a local market, and supplement with some favorite sides. Christmas a number of years back I told everyone I wanted to do the whole dinner myself, my way, and I took great joy in creating an Italian feast everyone loved. Every year since, we've done a meal from a different country, and best of all, my now-adult son cooks with me.

I think the trick with all these holiday issues is, stop trying to satisfy everyone else and decide to satisfy yourself. Kick Norman Rockwell and Martha Stewart to the curb, and invite imperfection and gratitude in.

Joy to the World

I admit I've become more than a bit "Bah Humbug" about Christmas. I've been that way for years now, and this year seemed like it would be even worse, with personal financial and other woes and the generally miserable state of the union and the world. Not exchanging gifts with friends and family because we didn't need more stuff yielded this year to not exchanging gifts because I'm too broke. All three holiday parties I'd looked forward to in December ended up being rescheduled until January for various reasons. I wasn't the only one not feelin' it. As one of my friends posted on her Facebook page, with all the busyness and added burden, "I will be glad when the holidays are over." As another put it, "We're all running around trying to make everything so special, we're not making it peaceful."

But lo and behold, I've gotten my Christmas spirit back. I put up a tree, and even decorated the house a bit. I watched "Christmas in Washington" on TV. I listened in the car to my all-time favorite holiday CD, Etta James *12 Songs of Christmas*.

Best of all, I went to a drive-through winter lights show with my friend Elsie and her young goddaughter, my goddaughter Annabelle. Both Elsie and I were weary from work, but we wanted to do "something holiday" together. We went out for a casual dinner first, and Annabelle was her usual delightful self. She generously offered to share her stuffed animal puppy Rudolph with me (her mom explained she had named quite a number of stuffed animals Rudolph recently). As has become a tradition with us each time we get together, Annabelle reached magically into her pocket and pulled out stickers for me, then carefully placed them on my sweater, and never has any expensive gift meant more to me than the love of those little fingers patting down an odd assortment of stickers. They were treasures to her, and I received them as such.

She also gave me a Christmas card she had created for me including even more stickers, with two new photos tucked in, one of her with Santa. She opened the paperback books I got her for Christmas with gratifying excitement (they featured various favorite characters enjoying snowy days—I'd gone in circles for nearly two hours in the children's section of the bookstore trying to find just the right ones). Later, as we walked back to the car (well, I walked, she skipped) with her hand in mine, she told me she had been dreaming about me. I told her I dream about her, too.

From the turnoff into the state park to the light show entrance was a bit of a drive, and the lights didn't start right away. Annabelle pronounced the dark forest "spooky," prompting her mother to ask, "Spooky good or spooky bad?" Without waiting for a response, we switched to distraction mode—Elsie making a funny ghost noise and I riffing on something, I don't even remember what—I said it was "RIDICULOUS." Both of these things tickled her no end, and for the next hour of our excursion she begged her mother to make the noise and me to say "RIDICULOUS!" each time setting her off into peals of laughter.

I reached into the bag I'd brought and pulled out an M&M cookie for each of us. As I passed one back to Miss A. in her car seat, her mother looked at me and said in alarm, "She doesn't like those," and as her daughter's little mouth turned down and she shook her head in disappointment, I mentally kicked myself, knowing I'd had other flavors of cookies I could have brought instead. Sucker! They both started beaming and I knew I'd been had in an impromptu mother-daughter skit.

Once the cookies and then clementines I'd also brought had been distributed and devoured, Annabelle asked if there were any more of the cookies. I told I was sorry, but no, all I had left was water. (I got credit from her mom for having thought ahead to her disinclination to load A. up on too much sugar at night.) She hopefully asked if I had anymore surprises ,and again I said, "Just water." L-o-n-g pause, followed by an emphatic declaration from the back seat, "I LOVE water!" I duly passed it back and she guzzled it down like it was elixir.

We continued on our merry way at two miles an hour through the lights of Teddy Bear Land, oohing and aahing at lit swans on the lake, and nutcracker soldiers standing at attention. The Subaru's tushy warmers were on, we were giddy and giggly, and we sang along to a radio station playing 24/7 Christmas carols. Annabelle informed me that she didn't get to see me enough; I agreed wholeheartedly, and we decided that we should talk on the phone more often. She pressed her mother to be sure and write my number down for her so she could call me herself.

Such pure joy in these moments when they occurred, and every time I remember them a smile breaks unbidden across my face.

The next day I had a nice talk with my dad on the phone, catching up. I called and swapped a few stories with my mom a bit later. Then I went to a get-together for Christmas cookies and conversation with friends in front of a lovingly decorated tree and roaring fire, and the moon came up nearly full, before sunset, as we approached the winter solstice.

I didn't stay too late, as I was meeting my son for dinner, always a treat.

Life is good.

Through the years
We all will be together,
If the Fates allow
Hang a shining star upon the highest bough.
And have yourself a merry little Christmas now.

1) "The middle zone of expectation of what will or should be and what is is indeed one of the great gray areas of life, and living there with grace and acceptance leads us to a far better quality of life than one constantly ruminating on what should be or what might have been."

Is there an area of your life in which you live in the zone of expectation, what will or should be? What does that make you feel when your expectations are not met? If you could change your perspective and accept what is instead, how would that affect that area of your life and your emotions around it?

2) The author identifies some of the aspects of "grace" as divine energy, spirit, graciousness, acceptance, kindness (to ourselves as well as others), and forgiveness.

Do you feel yours is a grace-filled life? If so, what about it fills and replenishes it with grace? How does that grace affect how you live your life and connect with others? If not, what can you do to bring more grace into your every-day living?

3) Kullgren's essay about paradigm shifts says her own biggest transformational shift came in "a series of quiet but important ones rather than in an epiphany." In her case, part of her shift was the recognition of herself as an optimistic person and a desire to live in congruence with that perspective.

Look back and identify a paradigm shift in your life. How did it transform you? What did you have to do and what are you still doing to facilitate the transformation? Did it open new possibilities for you?

READERSGUIDE

4) Kullgren ponders "do-overs" in one of her essays, including examples of a friend who went out and bought the same car she'd just had an accident in, and one woman who said her do-over would have been not to let her mother dissuade her from becoming a professional actor.

What are some do-overs you'd like to see in your life? Is there one big or small you could still really do something about? Give yourself the gift of a do-over.

5) The author says that adversity can bring blessings into our lives, even if we may not recognize them at the time. These blessings include rebirth, a call to change, increased mindfulness, a renewal of compassion, gratitude, and acceptance.

Have you had a period of adversity in your life, perhaps a health challenge, the death of a loved one, a work crisis, a loss of a romantic relationship, financial woes? Have you been able to see any blessings in your adversity or are they still waiting to reveal themselves?

6) One theme in Grace in the Gray Areas *is the curse of our speeded up lives, which harms both our physical and mental health. We multitask to the detriment of our own sanity and productivity, we are constantly on the go and afflicted with what some wear like a badge of honor—"crazy busyness," we are being bombarded with information. As Gandhi said, "There is more to life than increasing its speed."*

What steps can you take to slow down your life to make time for reflection, for attention, for mindfulness as you go about your day? How can you practice discernment amidst the constant flow of information from your phone, your computer, your TV, social media?

READERSGUIDE

7) The author tells us she is a passionate library lover, and she is a voracious reader.

What memories do you have of a favorite library in your life? Describe the physical environment, the "aura," the people coming and going. Think back to some beloved books. To what magical places did they take you? Do you still frequent a library and lose yourself in books?

8) Kullgren takes an unflinching look at her own body and talks about women's body image and aging in two of her essays.

Take a look at your own body and catalog what each part looks like and what you like and don't like about it. What is aging doing to your body and how do you feel about it? What if you were to remove all feelings of "like" and "don't like" and just accept what is? Remember, as the author quotes writer Anne Lamott, "Joy is the best makeup. Joy, and good lighting."

9) Family and friends are a constant undercurrent in Grace in the Gray Areas, *and are the source of many gray areas in our lives as we pull and tug between "hate" and love. We show wildly varying levels of grace as we inevitably march the path of turning into our mothers. We (hopefully) grow in compassion for our flawed parents as we age ourselves. We endure decades of high expectations of holidays met by imperfect implementation with our loved ones. We parent our children constantly floating between black and white and only hoping that parenting in the gray areas will be "good enough." Our friends keep us sane.*

Think about your relationship with a family member with whom you'd characterize your relationship as in the gray areas. Someone you love but who knows how to really push your buttons. How can you get some more grace in the gray areas of that relationship?

READERSGUIDE

10) With great humor the author examines our relationship with our physical possessions, our "stuff"–getting it, keeping it, loving it, hating it, dragging it around with us, and letting it go.

Now take a look at some other kind of "stuff" in your life—intangible stuff like disappointment, resentment, anger, perfectionism. We can love surrounding ourselves with these as much as our physical stuff. But there always comes a time to declutter. How will you take something that is not serving you anymore and discard it from the closet of your soul? Does it go in the "Save," "Donate," "Recycle," or "Trash" box?

11) In the chapter "Encounters with Grace" the author shares transformational arts experiences, and encounters with interesting people.

Have you had an encounter with grace lately? It can be anything from a walk with your dog to a concert to your child's graduation to a spiritual experience to a colorful sunset. Think about what imbued it with grace. Do you want more encounters with grace? How will you go out (or in) and get them?

Karen Kullgren is a freelance writer and editor with a particular interest in exploring women's lives, spiritual journeys, diverse cultures, and the universality of human experience. Her articles have been published in print and online in many local and national magazines and newspapers.

She is Contributing Editor for *Washington Parent* and was Contributing Editor for *Washington Woman*, where her "Grace in the Gray Areas" column appeared monthly.

Kullgren lives in the Maryland suburbs of Washington, DC and is the mother of one son.

Blogging at karenkullgren.blogspot.com, at www.facebook.com/graceinthegrayareas and on twitter @gracengrayareas, she also offers Journaling to Grace in the Gray Areas workshops.

www.ingramcontent.com/pod-product-compliance
Lightning Source LLC
Chambersburg PA
CBHW020620120726
47905CB00003B/866
* 9 7 8 0 9 9 6 2 3 9 8 0 6 *